I0430207

Assessment of Soil Amplification of Earthquake Ground Motion Using the "CARES" Code Version 1.2

U.S. Nuclear Regulatory Commission
Office Nuclear Reactor Regulation
Washington, DC 20555-0001

AVAILABILITY OF REFERENCE MATERIALS
IN NRC PUBLICATIONS

NRC Reference Material

As of November 1999, you may electronically access NUREG-series publications and other NRC records at NRC's Public Electronic Reading Room at www.nrc.gov/NRC/ADAMS/index.html.
Publicly released records include, to name a few, NUREG-series publications; *Federal Register* notices; applicant, licensee, and vendor documents and correspondence; NRC correspondence and internal memoranda; bulletins and information notices; inspection and investigative reports; licensee event reports; and Commission papers and their attachments.

NRC publications in the NUREG series, NRC regulations, and *Title 10, Energy*, in the Code of *Federal Regulations* may also be purchased from one of these two sources.
1. The Superintendent of Documents
   U.S. Government Printing Office
   Mail Stop SSOP
   Washington, DC 20402–0001
   Internet: bookstore.gpo.gov
   Telephone: 202-512-1800
   Fax: 202-512-2250
2. The National Technical Information Service
   Springfield, VA 22161–0002
   www.ntis.gov
   1–800–553–6847 or, locally, 703–605–6000

A single copy of each NRC draft report for comment is available free, to the extent of supply, upon written request as follows:
Address: Office of the Chief Information Officer,
          Reproduction and Distribution
          Services Section
          U.S. Nuclear Regulatory Commission
          Washington, DC 20555-0001
E-mail: DISTRIBUTION@nrc.gov
Facsimile: 301–415–2289

Some publications in the NUREG series that are posted at NRC's Web site address www.nrc.gov/NRC/NUREGS/indexnum.html are updated periodically and may differ from the last printed version. Although references to material found on a Web site bear the date the material was accessed, the material available on the date cited may subsequently be removed from the site.

Non-NRC Reference Material

Documents available from public and special technical libraries include all open literature items, such as books, journal articles, and transactions, *Federal Register* notices, Federal and State legislation, and congressional reports. Such documents as theses, dissertations, foreign reports and translations, and non-NRC conference proceedings may be purchased from their sponsoring organization.

Copies of industry codes and standards used in a substantive manner in the NRC regulatory process are maintained at—
          The NRC Technical Library
          Two White Flint North
          11545 Rockville Pike
          Rockville, MD 20852–2738

These standards are available in the library for reference use by the public. Codes and standards are usually copyrighted and may be purchased from the originating organization or, if they are American National Standards, from—
          American National Standards Institute
          11 West 42nd Street
          New York, NY 10036–8002
          www.ansi.org
          212–642–4900

Legally binding regulatory requirements are stated only in laws; NRC regulations; licenses, including technical specifications; or orders, not in NUREG-series publications. The views expressed in contractor-prepared publications in this series are not necessarily those of the NRC.

The NUREG series comprises (1) technical and administrative reports and books prepared by the staff (NUREG–XXXX) or agency contractors (NUREG/CR–XXXX), (2) proceedings of conferences (NUREG/CP–XXXX), (3) reports resulting from international agreements (NUREG/IA–XXXX), (4) brochures (NUREG/BR–XXXX), and (5) compilations of legal decisions and orders of the Commission and Atomic and Safety Licensing Boards and of Directors' decisions under Section 2.206 of NRC's regulations (NUREG–0750).

Assessment of Soil Amplification of Earthquake Ground Motion Using the "CARES" Code Version 1.2

Manuscript Completed: September 2001
Date Published: September 2001

Prepared by
R. Pichumani

Division of Engineering
Office of Nuclear Reactor Regulation
U.S. Nuclear Regulatory Commission
Washington, DC 20555-0001

ABSTRACT

This report describes the results of two studies to assess the soil amplification of earthquake ground motion by varying three parameters pertinent to the soil and rock supporting nuclear power plant structures. Both studies used version 1.2 of the computer code CARES, Version 1.0 of which was developed by Brookhaven National Laboratory for the U.S. Nuclear Regulatory Commission. The model is a single layer of soil overlying a rock half-space. In the first study, the input earthquake ground motion (corresponding to the Regulatory Guide1.60 spectrum) was specified at the rock level. The parameters varied in the first study were: the shear wave velocity of the soil stratum, the thickness of the soil stratum, and the shear wave velocity of the rock half-space underlying the soil stratum. The study analyzed the effects of varying each parameter on the motion at the ground surface and at 40 feet (ft) below the ground surface. Three values of soil layer thickness were considered: 50 ft, 100 ft, and 200 ft. Three values of the shear wave velocity of the soil stratum were considered, 1000 ft per second (fps), 2000 fps, and 3000 fps. The three shear wave velocities of the rock were 5000 fps, 7500 fps, and 10000 fps. The results of the first parametric study show significant shifts in the frequency at which the maximum spectral acceleration occurs when the soil thickness is varied from 50 ft to 200 ft and when the shear wave velocity of the soil stratum is varied from 1000 fps to 3000 fps.

No frequency shifts are seen when the shear wave velocity of the rock medium is varied from 5000 fps to 10000 fps, but significant changes in the maximum spectral amplitude of acceleration are observed for the 100 ft and 200 ft thick soil layer. The second parametric study used the seismic ground motion specified by a rock site-specific spectra input at the rock outcrop, varying only the thickness of the soil layer and the shear wave velocity of the soil layer. A comparison of the results of the two parametric studies shows that the shapes of the spectral responses for both types of ground motion input are quite similar to the corresponding cases of soil thickness and soil shear wave velocity. However, the spectral amplitudes obtained for the site-specific rock spectra input are lower than the corresponding values for the Regulatory Guide (R.G)1.60 input because the amplitudes of the input spectral accelerations of the site-specific rock spectra are lower than those of the R.G. 1.60 spectra at all frequencies larger than approximately 0.18 Hz, even though the peak ground acceleration (PGA) of the site-specific rock spectra was set at 0.3g by scaling the actual PGA of 0.24g by a factor of 1.25 to match the 0.3g PGA of the R.G. 1.60 spectra.

CONTENTS

TABLES

FIGURES

ACKNOWLEDGMENTS

This parametric study to assess the soil amplification of earthquake ground motion was performed using the computer code CARES, Version 1.2. Version 1.0 of CARES was originally developed by Brookhaven National Laboratory (BNL) for the Office of Nuclear Regulatory Research (RES), U.S. Nuclear Regulatory Commission (NRC), and published in July 1990 (NUREG/CR-5588, Volumes 1, 2, and 3). Herman Graves III of RES was the NRC Project Manager in charge of developing the original CARES code. CARES Version 1.2 was the result of modifications and additions made to Version 1.0 by Carl J. Costantino, Charles A. Miller, Ernest Heymsfield, and Anshi Yang for the Office of Nuclear Reactor Regulation (NRR), U.S. NRC. The author acknowledges the support and advice of Robert Rothman, Goutam Bagchi, Eugene Imbro, and Kamal Manoly of the Office of NRR.

ABBREVIATIONS

ADAMS	Agency Wide Documents Access and Management System
BNL	Brookhaven National Laboratory
fps	Feet per second
ft	Feet
g	Acceleration due to gravity
H	Thickness
IMSL	A graphics plotting software program
NRC	U.S. Nuclear Regulatory Commission
NRR	(Office of) Nuclear Reactor Regulation, U.S. NRC
RES	(Office of) Nuclear Regulatory Research, U.S. NRC
R.G.	Regulatory Guide
ROC	Rock outcrop
v	Version
V_R	Shear wave velocity of Rock
V_R5	$V_R = 5000$ fps
$V_R7.5$	$V_R = 7500$ fps
V_R10	$V_R = 10,000$ fps
V_s	Shear wave velocity of soil
V_s1	$V_s = 1000$ fps
V_s2	$V_s = 2000$ fps
V_s3	$V_s = 3000$ fps

1. INTRODUCTION

To perform the seismic analysis of a structure, an appropriate seismic demand is needed. Seismic demands are generally in the form of earthquake time histories or earthquake ground motion spectra. The demands should reflect the seismic hazard at the site of the structure with a level of conservatism appropriate to the function of the structure. Seismic demands can be developed by using theoretical numerical models or empirical earthquake data or a combination of the two. The seismic demand should be based on the magnitude of the earthquake and its distance from the site, the geology between the sources and the site, and the conditions at the immediate site. For sites founded on soils, there is often not enough strong-ground-motion data available from similar sites to make a statistically robust estimate of the seismic demand. In such cases, it is common to estimate the seismic ground motion at the site by assuming that the site geology is rock. The rock ground motion is then used as input to a computer model of the soil column, which represents the actual geology at the site, to obtain the seismic demand to be used for the design or analysis of the civil structure. The study reported here investigated the sensitivity of the seismic hazard using the computer code CARES (Computer Analysis for Rapid Evaluation of Structures), version 1.2 (Ref. 1), by performing two sets of parametric evaluations of the effects of the properties of the soil and the underlying rock that support the structures. Two kinds of seismic ground motion input (one specified by Regulatory Guide (R.G.) 1.60 spectrum, the other specified by a site-specific rock spectrum) were applied at the rock outcrop, and the results of the soil amplification of the earthquake ground motion were compared for both cases of seismic hazard.

2. OVERVIEW OF CARES CODE

Background

During the late 1980s, the CARES computer program was developed for the Nuclear Regulatory Commission (NRC) by Brookhaven National Laboratory. The first version of the CARES code (Ref. 2) was designed for use on a small personal computer (PC) and was intended to provide the NRC staff with the capability to rapidly evaluate the seismic response of simplified structural stick models of nuclear power plant structures. This capability enabled the staff to quickly check the validity and/or accuracy of the analytical data received from applicants for nuclear power plant licensing actions. These data were typically obtained from numerical studies performed with large state-of-the-art computer packages for structural analysis and were difficult to assess. By performing simplified analytical model studies, the staff could evaluate the sensitivity of computed responses to variations in a host of controlling parameters to confirm the results of studies done with the larger computers.

Since the original development, the staff has validated the usefulness of the CARES concept by applying it to a number of problems. The CARES code has been modified to operate on the Sun SPARC workstations. The code is modular, which allows the user to access various capabilities in an interactive fashion. The code has three primary functions (Refs. 1 and 2):

> a. A free-field computational algorithm allows the analysis of the seismic response of a layered soil column subjected to upwardly propagating horizontal shear waves developed by a given input seismic motion. The input motion can be specified by a target response spectrum appropriate tor a given earthquake magnitude at a given distance from the source or by an actual accelerogram at a given location in the soil column. The algorithm computes the motion at various locations in the soil column for the input seismic motion as well as the final stress and strain conditions developed in each soil layer.

> b. From the ground motions generated in the free-field analysis module above, the seismic response of a structure embedded in or supported by the soil can be determined.

> c. A variety of postprocessing capabilities allow the generation of other parameters of interest in the dynamic response (soil motions at any depth of interest to the user, in-structure response spectra, etc.) and plotting of results.

The capability to easily perform simplified analyses at one's desk on a PC has proved to be a valuable asset. As always, however, advances in the state of the art of seismic response calculations made it desirable to expand the capability of the CARES code. In addition, the staff wanted to tackle bigger problems with CARES because the new structural stick models in the advanced reactor programs were significantly larger than the models used in the original CARES development. The CARES code was therefore extended and modified to satisfy these new objectives, resulting in CARES version (v) 1.1.

A version of CARES v 1.1 designated as CARES v 1.2, was developed to run on Sun SPARC workstations, which operate in the UNIX environment. CARES v 1.2 (Ref. 1) runs only on the SPARC workstation, although it can be made operational on other machines with minor reprogramming. To further utilize the capabilities of the workstation, CARES v 1.2 modifies and extends to take advantage of the plotting capability of CARES v 1.1, i.e., the IMSL plotting software appropriate to the Sun workstation. On-line plots of computed results can be obtained in this new version and then be saved or printed.

Two major changes were incorporated in CARES v 1.1 to extend the capability of the code. The first change allowed the inclusion of a rock outcrop model within the soil column formulation. Second, extended soil modulus degradation models were incorporated to keep pace with recent developments. In CARES v 1.2, the computations have been extended to include calculation of tau/sigma stress ratios for soil liquefaction evaluations. Improvements have also been added to the soil degradation specification in the code, as has the code's ability to output initial and final soil properties in the convolution calculations.

Program Modules

The CARES code performs three separate functions: the free-field analysis, the structural (or soil-structure interaction) analysis, and the ancillary or pre- and post-processing analyses of ground motion time histories or spectra. In the original PC-based version, CARES v 1.0, the program essentially had a single "general manager," which allowed the transfer of data between any and all of the individual modules directly accessed by the code. This was no longer possible with the greatly expanded capability of v 1.1. Each of the free-field and structural modules were significantly larger, making the use of a single General Manager impractical. Therefore, CARES v 1.1 was divided into modules. V 1.2 maintains the separate modules and has a common input/output file format to allow easy communication between the modules. The modules are labeled CRSSOIL, CRSSTRUC, CRSPOST, and CRSPLOT. Data transfer is accomplished by using data files generated by each module and stored on the disk. Data entry is described in Section 3 of Ref. 1 and can be easily performed using the machine prompts for interactive operation of the code.

3. PARAMETRIC STUDIES AND RESULTS

Two parametric studies were performed by varying the significant properties of the foundation materials for two kinds of seismic ground motion input (i.e., one specified by R.G. 1.60 spectra, the other by site-specific rock spectrum) applied at the rock outcrop. Three parameters were varied in the first study:

1. the thickness, H, in feet (ft), of the soil layer
2. the shear wave velocity of the soil layer, V_s
3. the shear wave velocity of the rock underlying the soil stratum, V_R

Table 1 lists the values of these three parameters that were varied in this study. For each of the three values of thickness, H, of the soil stratum (50 ft, 100 ft, and 200 ft), three values of V_s (1000 fps, 2000 fps, and 3000 fps) and three values of V_R (5000 fps, 7500 fps, and 10000 fps) were used; so there were 27 computer analyses. In all 27 runs, the seismic ground motion was input at the rock outcrop as the spectral acceleration value of the R.G. 1.60 spectrum with a peak ground acceleration (PGA) of 0.3g, and convolved up through the soil stratum using the CRSSOIL segment of the CARES code.

In the second parametric study, nine analyses (varying V_s and H as with the R.G. 1.60 input, but keeping V_R constant) were performed using a site-specific rock spectra input for seismic ground motion at the rock outcrop with a PGA of 0.24g scaled by 1.25 to match the 0.3g PGA of The R.G. 1.60 spectrum.

Results for R.G. 1.60 Input

The convolution analyses of seismic ground motion for the 27 combinations of the three parameters provided the ground motions at the ground surface of the soil and at a depth of 40 ft below the ground surface with the input seismic ground motion specified at the rock outcrop (ROC). One general finding is that the maximum motions at the ground surface are larger than 40 ft below the ground surface for all combinations of the three parameters. However, the amplitudes and the frequency of maximum amplitude at these elevations differed significantly for various values of the three parameters considered in this study.

These observations are confirmed by the results of additional postprocessing of the basic output data from the 27 cases. The additional postprocessing was done to illustrate the effects of the three parameters (H, V_s, and V_R) on the amplifications and frequency characteristics of the ground motions at the two depths. Table 2 shows the combinations of the parameters used in these postprocessing computer runs. The effects are shown in Figures 1 through 18.

Figures 1 and 2 show the effects of using the three values of soil thickness, H, on the amplitude at the surface and 40 feet below the surface. The two figures show that the frequency dramatically decreases as the soil thickness increases from 50 ft to 100 ft and to 200 ft, keeping V_s at 2000 fps and V_R at 10000 fps. Figure 1 shows that the maximum spectral amplitude of acceleration at the ground surface *increases* from about 3.3g to about 3.65g as the soil layer thickness *increases from 50 ft to 100 ft*, but *decreases* from about 3.65g to about 2.9g as the soil layer thickness *increases from 100 ft to 200 ft*. Figure 2 shows similar increase in frequency and decrease in spectral amplitude in the response spectra at 40 ft below the ground surface.

4

Figures 3 and 4 show frequency shifts in the maximum spectral acceleration when the soil shear wave velocity, V_s, is varied from 1000 fps to 3000 fps, keeping the thickness of the soil layer, H, at 100 ft and the rock shear wave velocity, V_R, at 10000 fps. The frequency at which the maximum spectral amplitude of acceleration occurs increases with increasing values of the soil layer shear wave velocity, V_s. The spectral amplitude increases as V_s increases from 1000 fps to 2000 fps, but decreases when Vs increases from 2000 fps to 3000 fps.

Figures 5 and 6 show the effect of using rock shear wave velocities of 5000, 7500, and 10000 fps and keeping the soil layer thickness at 100 ft and the soil layer shear wave velocity at 2000 fps. In this case, the maximum spectral amplitude of accelerations increases significantly with increasing values of rock shear wave velocity, both at the ground surface and 40 ft below the ground surface. However, there are no frequency shifts for any of the three values of rock shear wave velocity.

Figures 7 and 8 show the effect of the soil thickness 50 ft, 100 ft, and 200 ft with soil and rock velocities of 1000 fps and 10,000 fps, respectively. The frequency at which maximum spectral amplitude of acceleration occurs decreases with increasing soil thickness, as in the case of V_s=2000 fps and V_R=10,000 fps (Figs.1 and 2). The maximum spectral amplitude at the ground surface for a 50 ft thick soil layer is significantly higher (about 3.4g) than for the 100 ft thick soil (about 2.1g).

Figures 9 and 10 show the effect of varying the values of soil shear wave velocity (V_s) from 1000 fps to 2000 fps and 3000 fps for a 50 ft thick soil layer overlying a rock half-space with the shear wave velocity of the rock (V_R) at 10,000 fps. The frequency at which the maximum spectral amplitude of accelerations occurs increases with increasing V_s as in the case of 100 ft thick soil in Figures 3 and 4; however, the maximum spectral amplitude decreases with increasing V_s contrary to the case of 100 ft thick soil.

Figures 11 and 12 show the effect of using V_R values of 5000 fps, 7500 fps, and 10,000 fps, keeping the soil layer thickness at 50 ft and V_s at 1000 fps. There is no change in the frequency at which the maximum spectral amplitude of acceleration occurs. The shapes of the spectral curves are similar. There is an increase in the maximum spectral amplitude at the ground surface from about 3g for V_R = 5000 fps to about 3.5g for V_R=10000 fps, as seen in Figure 11. Figure 12 shows similar results for 40 ft below the ground surface, with maximum spectral amplitudes increasing from about 1.5g for V_R = 5000 fps to about 1.7g for V_R = 10000 fps.

Figures 13 and 14 show the effect of soil thickness on spectral acceleration when the soil shear wave velocity is 3000 fps and the rock shear wave velocity is 10000 fps. Comparing the spectral curves shown in Figure 13 with those in Figure 7 (which gives the results for V_s=1000 and V_R = 10000 fps), the following are noted:

1. The frequencies at which the maximum spectral amplitude of accelerations occurs decrease with increasing soil thickness in both cases (for V_s = 1000 fps and V_s = 3000 fps). However, the frequency at which the maximum spectral amplitude occurs for V_s = 3000 fps and H = 50 ft is about 12 Hz, whereas the corresponding frequency for soil with V_s = 1000 fps is about 3 Hz. Similar decreases in the frequencies at which the maximum acceleration occurs are also noted for H = 100 ft and 200 ft .

2. The maximum spectral amplitude for the soil layer with V_s = 1000 fps (in Figure 7) is significantly higher for H=50 ft than the corresponding amplitude for the soil layer with V_s = 3000 fps (Figures 7 and 13). However, the maximum spectral

amplitudes for the 100 ft and 200 ft thick soil strata are higher for the higher velocity soil than the corresponding amplitude for the lower velocity soil.

Figures 15 and 16 show the effect of using the soil shear wave velocities, V_s, of 1000 fps, 2000 fps, and 3000 fps for a soil thickness of 200 ft and a rock shear wave velocity of 10000 fps. Comparing the spectral curves in Figures 15 and 16 (for H = 200 ft) with those in Figures 3 and 4 (for H = 100 ft) shows that the maximum spectral amplitude of accelerations occurs at lower frequencies for H = 200 ft than for H = 100 ft. Furthermore, the maximum spectral amplitudes for the 100 ft thick soil are larger for V_s = 1000 fps and 2000 fps than the corresponding amplitudes for the 200 ft thick soil. However, the maximum spectral amplitude for the 200 ft thick soil (with V_s = 3000 fps) is larger (about 3.05g) than the corresponding amplitude (about 2.85g) for the 100 ft thick soil (with V_s = 3000 fps), as seen in Figures 3 and 15.

Figures 17 and 18 show the effect of using values of rock shear wave velocity, V_R, of 5000 fps, 7500 fps, and 10000 fps for soil layer thickness of 200 ft and V_s = 3000 fps. The variations in rock shear wave velocities from 5000 fps to 10000 fps produce negligible change in the frequencies at which the maximum spectral amplitudes occur both at ground surface and at 40ft below ground surface. However, the maximum spectral amplitude at ground surface is about 50% larger for rock with V_R = 10000 fps than for rock with V_R = 5000 fps (Figure 17). Similar (qualitative) phenomena are also seen in Figure 5 and 6 for a 100 ft thick soil stratum with minor variations in frequency and amplitudes.

Results for Site-Specific Rock Spectra

Table 3 lists the values of the soil parameters, H and V_s, that were combined in the second parametric study. Figures 19 through 30 show the results of the nine computer analyses performed using a site-specific rock spectrum input at the rock outcrop and varying the soil thickness and soil shear wave velocity (as with the case of R.G. 1.60 input), but keeping the rock shear wave velocity constant at 10,000 fps. These figures illustrate the effects of the two parameters (H and V_s) on the amplifications and frequency characteristics of the ground motions at the ground surface and at 40 ft below the ground surface. Table 4 shows the combinations of the parameters used in postprocessing the results of the second parametric study.

Comparing the ground motions due to site-specific rock spectra input at the rock outcrop shown in Figures 19 through 30 with the corresponding results obtained using the R.G.1.60 input shows that the shapes of the spectral responses for both types of ground motion input (with a PGA of 0.3g) are quite similar for the corresponding cases of soil thickness and the soil layer shear wave velocity. However, the maximum amplitudes of the spectral response accelerations for the site-specific rock spectra input are lower than the corresponding response values for the R.G. 1.60 spectra. The explanation may be that (as seen in Figure 31) the amplitudes of the input spectral accelerations of the site-specific rock spectra are lower than those of the R. G. 1.60 spectra at all frequencies larger than approximately 0.18 Hz, even though the PGA of the site-specific rock spectrum was set at 0.3g by scaling its actual PGA of 0.24g by a factor of 1.25 to match the PGA of 0.3g of the R.G. 1.60 spectrum.

4. SUMMARY

Two parametric studies were performed by varying the significant properties of the foundation materials for two kinds of seismic ground motion input (i.e., one specified by Regulatory Guide 1.60 spectrum, the other by a site-specific rock spectrum) applied at the rock outcrop. The studies examined the effects of varying three parameters of the soil and rock on the amplitude of ground motion response spectra due to seismic ground motion. Three parameters were varied in the first study:

1. thickness of the soil layer
2. shear wave velocity of the soil layer
3. shear wave velocity of the underlying rock half-space

This study analyzed the effects of varying each parameter on the response spectra at the ground surface and at 40 feet below the ground surface. The thicknesses of the foundation soil were 50 ft, 100 ft, and 200 ft. Three values of the shear wave velocity of the soil were considered: 1000 fps, 2000 fps, and 3000 fps. The values of the shear wave velocity of the rock were 5000 fps, 7500 fps, and 10000 fps. The results of the parametric study show significant shifts in the frequency at which the maximum spectral amplitude of acceleration occurs when the soil thickness is changed and also when the shear wave velocity of the soil layer is varied. No frequency shifts are seen when the shear wave velocity of the rock is varied from 5000 fps to 10000 fps, but significant changes in the maximum amplitude of the spectral acceleration are observed for soil thicknesses of 100 ft and 200 ft. The changes in the amplitude are not as significant for the 50 ft thick soil stratum as for the deeper soil strata.

The second study used the seismic ground motion specified by a rock site-specific spectrum input at the rock outcrop, varying only the thickness of the soil layer and the shear wave velocity of the soil layer. The shear wave velocity of the rock stratum underlying the soil layer was kept constant at 10,000fps. The values of the other two soil parameters in this second parametric study were the same as in the first set.

A comparison of the results of the two parametric studies shows that the shapes of the spectral responses for both types of ground motion input (with a PGA of 0.3g) are quite similar for the corresponding cases of soil thickness and the soil shear wave velocity. However, the maximum spectral amplitudes obtained for the site-specific rock spectra input are lower than the corresponding values for the Regulatory Guide1.60 input, because the amplitudes of the input spectral accelerations of the site-specific rock spectra are lower than those of the Regulatory Guide1.60 spectra at all frequencies larger than approximately 0.18 Hz, even though the PGA of the site-specific rock spectrum was set at 0.3g by scaling its actual PGA of 0.24g by a factor of 1.25 to match the 0.3g PGA of the Regulatory Guide1.60 spectrum.

5. CONCLUSION

The type of the seismic ground motion input spectrum does not affect the response of the soil layers overlying the rock stratum. Both types of ground motion input have similar qualitative effects on the frequencies and spectral amplitudes of ground motion. However, the quantitative values of the response spectral amplitudes in the case of the site-specific rock spectra are lower than for the Regulatory Guide1.60 spectra. The reason is that the amplitudes of the input spectral accelerations of the site-specific rock spectra are lower than those of the Regulatory Guide1.60 spectra at all frequencies larger than approximately 0.18 Hz, even though the PGA of the site-specific rock spectra was set at 0.3g by scaling the actual PGA of 0.24g by a factor of 1.25 to match the 0.3g PGA of the Regulatory Guide1.60 spectra.

6. REFERENCES

1. CARES - Computer Analysis for Rapid Evaluation of Structures, Version 1.2, report prepared by Carl J. Costantino, Charles A. Miller, Ernest Heymsfield, and Anshi Yang. (ADAMS Accession No. ML012670148).

2. CARES (Computer Analysis for Rapid Evaluation of Structures), Version 1.0, NUREG/CR-5588, Vols. 1 through 3 prepared by J. Xu, A.J. Philippacopoulas, C.A. Miller, and C. J. Costantino, Brookhaven National Laboratory, for U.S. Nuclear Regulatory Commission, July 1990.

Table 1. Parametric Variation of Soil Properties for R. G. 1.60 Spectrum (PGA 0.3g) Input at Rock Outcrop

Run No.	Depth of soil, ft	Soil Shear Wave Velocity	Rock Shear Wave Velocity
1	100	2000	7,500
2	100	2000	10,000
3	100	2000	5,000
4	200	2000	7,500
5	200	2000	10,000
6	200	2000	5,000
7	50	2000	7,500
8	50	2000	10,000
9	50	2000	5,000
10	50	1000	7,500
11	50	1000	10,000
12	50	1000	5,000
13	100	1000	7,500
14	100	1000	10,000
15	100	1000	5,000
16	200	1000	7,500
17	200	1000	10,000
18	200	1000	5000
19	50	3000	7,500
20	50	3000	10,000
21	50	3000	5,000
22	100	3000	7,500
23	100	3000	10,000
24	100	3000	5,000
25	200	3000	7,500
26	200	3000	10,000
27	200	3000	5,000

Table 2: Combinations of Parameters to Study the Effects of Soil and Rock Properties on Amplification for R.G. 1.60 Input

S. No.	Computer Run Nos. for amplifications @ 0 ft and 40ft	Soil thickness, H (ft)	Soil Shear Wave Velocity, V_s (fps)	Rock Shear Wave Velocity, V_r (fps)
1	1 and 2 (using Runs 2, 5, and 8)*	50, 100, 200	2000	10000
2	3 and 4 (using Runs 2, 14, and 23)	100	1000, 2000, 3000	10000
3	5 and 6 (using Runs 3, 1, and 2)	100	2000	5000, 7500, 10000
4	7 and 8 (using Runs 11, 14, and 17)	50, 100, 200	1000	10000
5	9 and 10 (using Runs 11, 8, and 20)	50	1000, 2000, 3000	10000
6	11 and 12 (using Runs 12, 10, and 11)	50	1000	5000, 7500, 10000
7	13 and 14 (using Runs 20, 23, and 26)	50, 100, 200	3000	10000
8	15 and 16 (using Runs 17, 5, and 26)	200	1000, 2000, 3000	10000
9	17 and 18 (using Runs 27, 25, and 26)	200	3000	5000, 7500, 10000

* Output of amplifications from the computer runs 1 through 27 shown in parentheses here and is used in CRSPLOT to plot the effects of various combinations of soil and rock properties on soil amplifications in Figures 1 through 18.

Table 3: Parametric Variation of Soil Properties for Site-Specific Rock Spectra (PGA 0.24g scaled by 1.25 to match the R. G. 1.60 PGA of 0.3g)

Run Nos.	Depth of Soil (H), ft	V_s, fps	Remarks
1	50	1000	V_R = 10,000fps for all runs in this set.
2	100	1000	
3	200	1000	
4	50	2000	
5	100	2000	
6	200	2000	
7	50	3000	
8	100	3000	
9	200	3000	

Table 4: Combinations of Parameters to Study the Effects of Soil and Rock Properties on Amplification for Site-Specific Rock Spectra (V_R = 10,000fps)

S. No.	Soil Thickness H, ft	Soil Shear Wave Velocity, V_s, fps	Remarks
1	50,100, 200	1000	Effect of Soil thickness for Vs=1000 fps
2	50	1000, 2000, 3000	Effect of Vs for H=50 ft
3	50,100, 200	2000	Effect of Soil thickness for Vs=2000 fps
4	100	1000, 2000, 3000	Effect of Vs for H=100 ft
5	50,100, 200	3000	Effect of Soil thickness for Vs=3000 fps
6	200	1000, 2000, 3000	Effect of Vs for H=200 ft

FIGURES

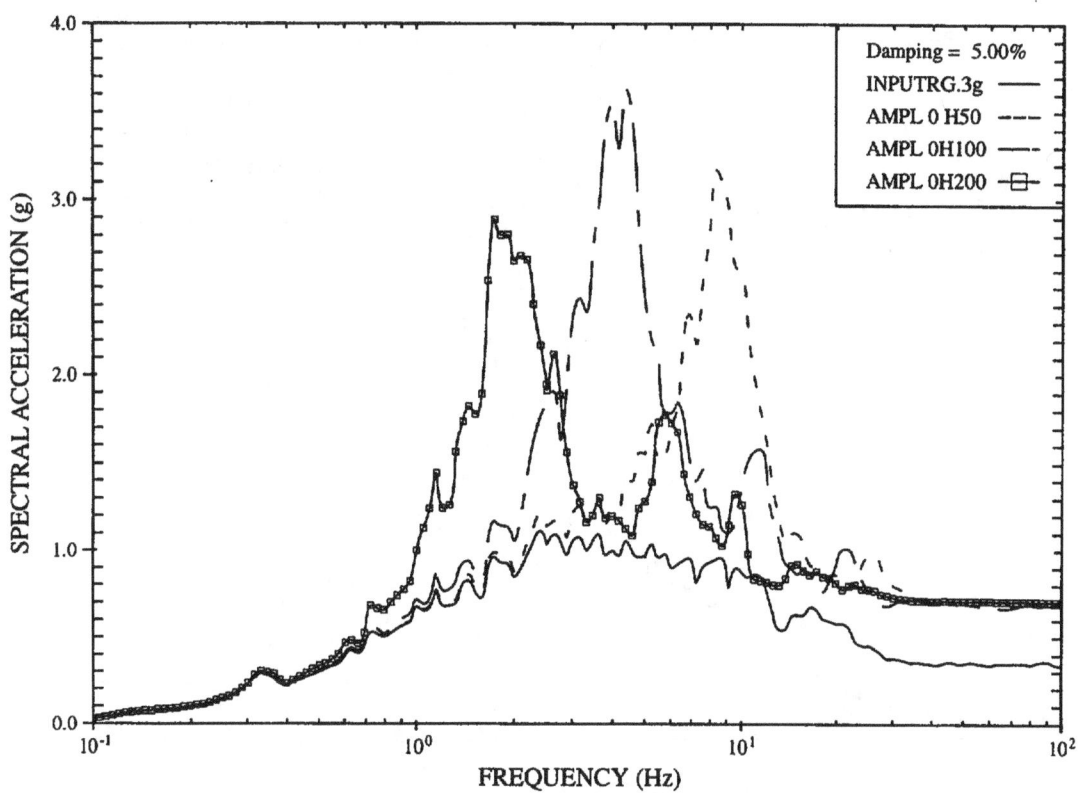

Figure 1. Effect of Soil Thickness, H, on Amplification at Ground Surface
(V_s=2000fps; V_R=10,000fps) for R.G. 1.60 Input

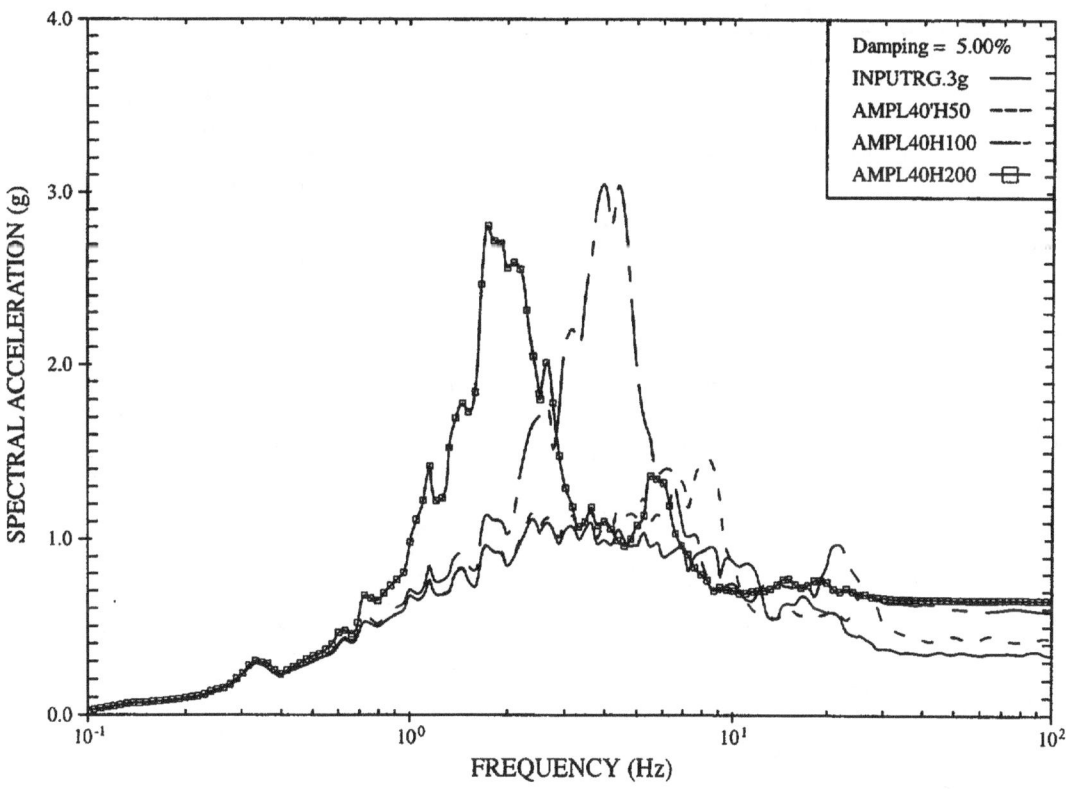

Figure 2. Effect of Soil Thickness, H, on Amplification at Depth of 40 ft
(V_s=2000fps; V_R=10,000fps) for R.G. 1.60 Input

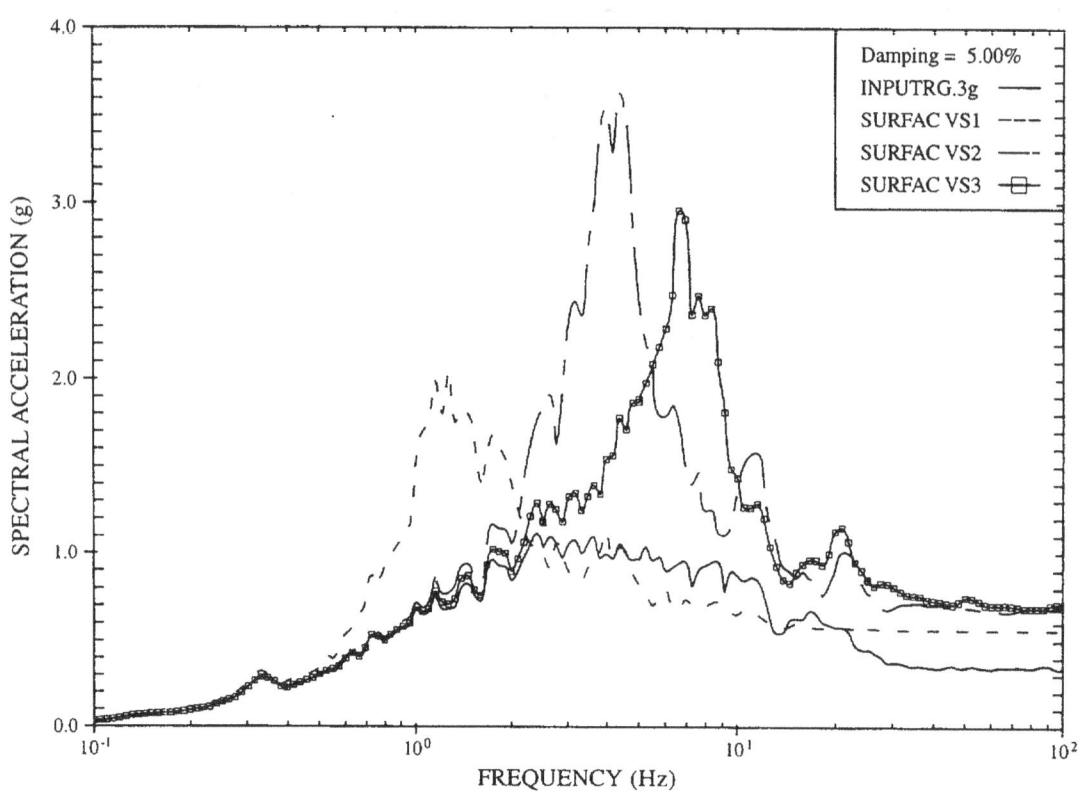

Figure 3. Effect of Soil Shear Wave Velocity, V_s, on Amplification at Ground Surface
(H=100ft; V_R=10,000fps) for R.G. 1.60 Input

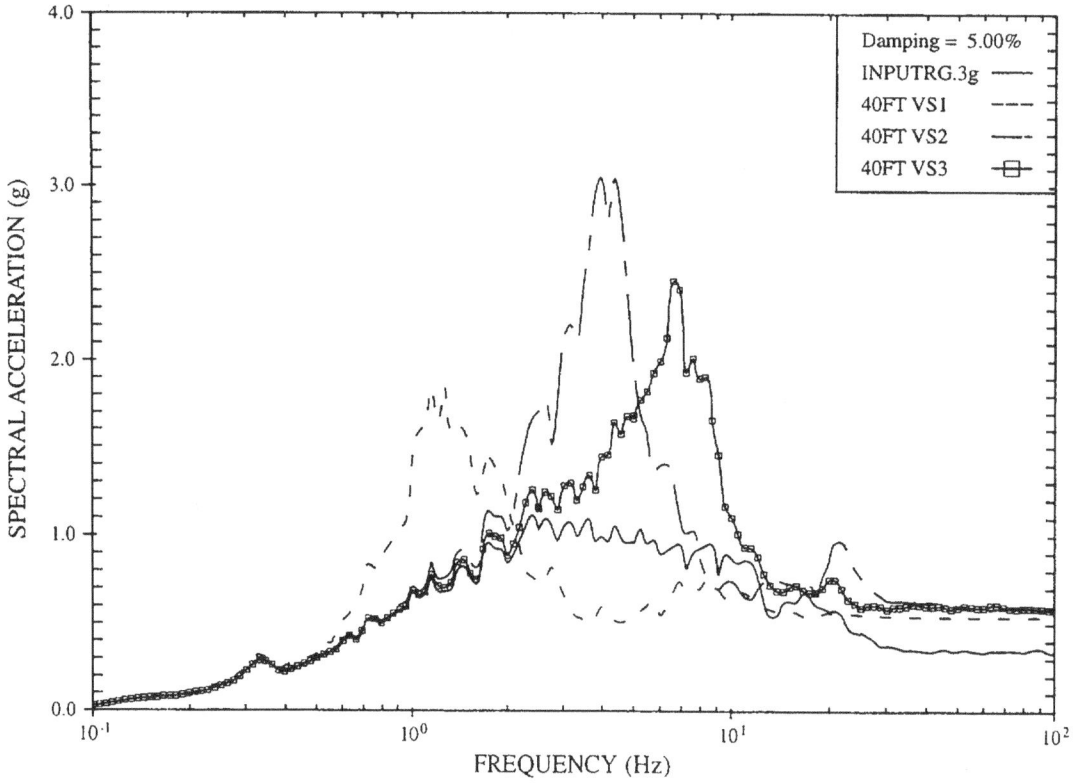

Figure 4. Effect of Soil Shear Wave Velocity, V_s, on Amplification at Depth of 40 ft
(H=100ft; V_R=10,000fps) for R.G. 1.60 Input

16

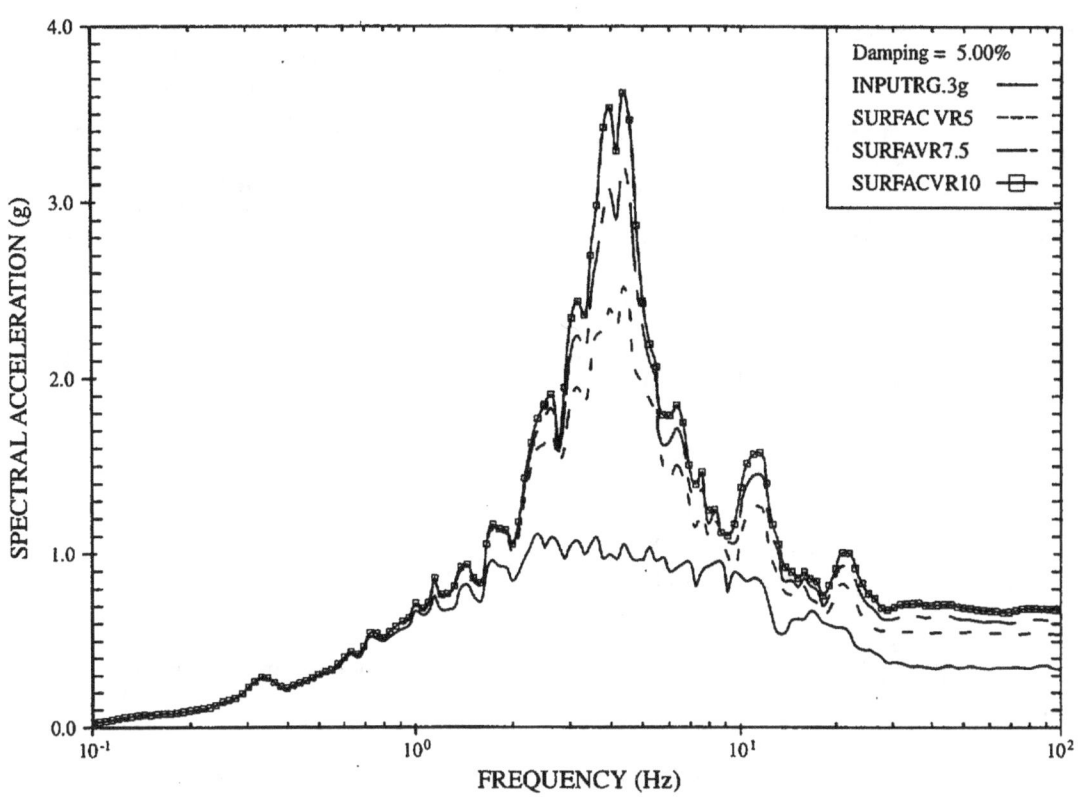

Figure 5. Effect of Rock Shear Wave Velocity, V_R, on Amplification at Ground Surface (H=100ft; V_s=2000fps) for R.G. 1.60 Input

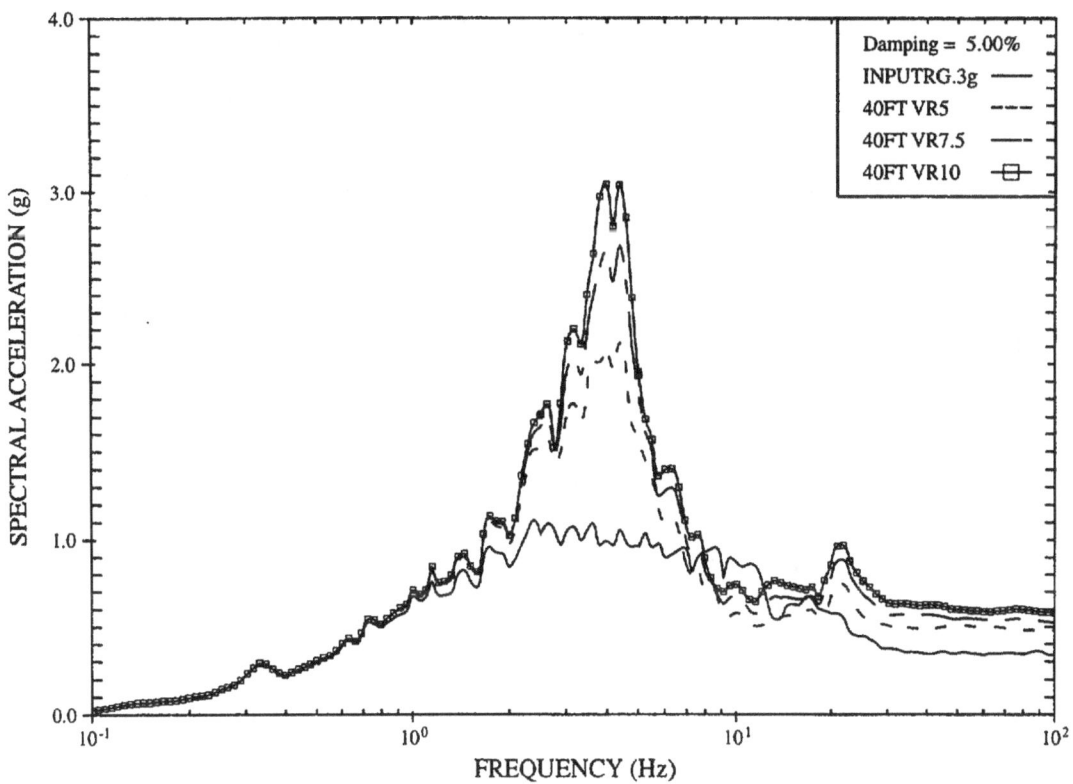

Figure 6. Effect of Rock Shear Wave Velocity, V_R, on Amplification at Depth of 40 ft (H=100ft; V_s=2000fps) for R.G. 1.60 Input

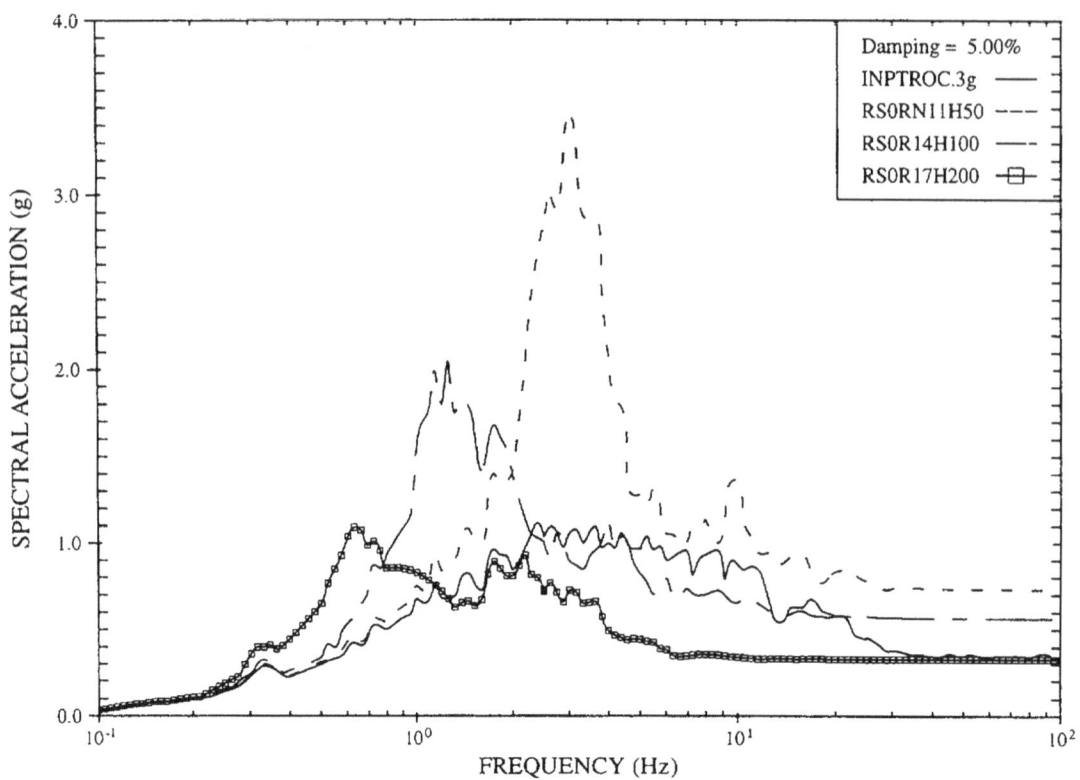

Figure 7. Effect of Soil Thickness on Amplification at Ground Surface
(V_s=1000fps; V_R=10,000fps) for R.G. 1.60 Input

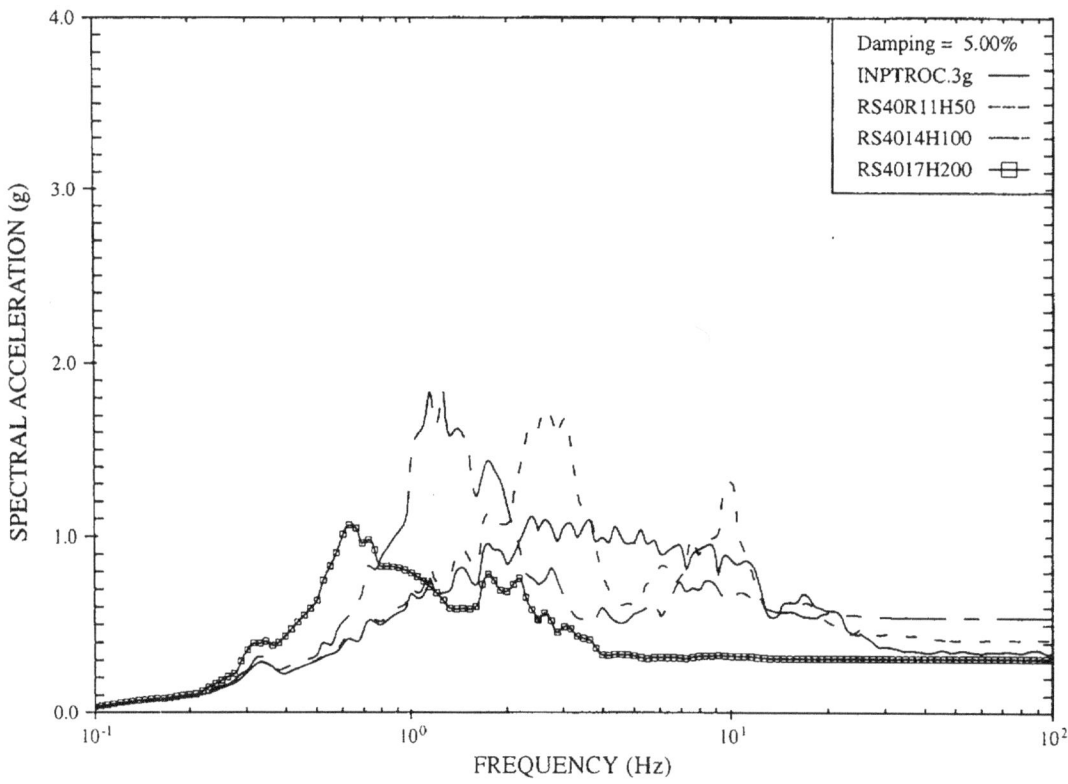

Figure 8. Effect of Soil Thickness on Amplification at Depth of 40 ft
(V_s=1000fps; V_R=10,000fps) for R.G. 1.60 Input

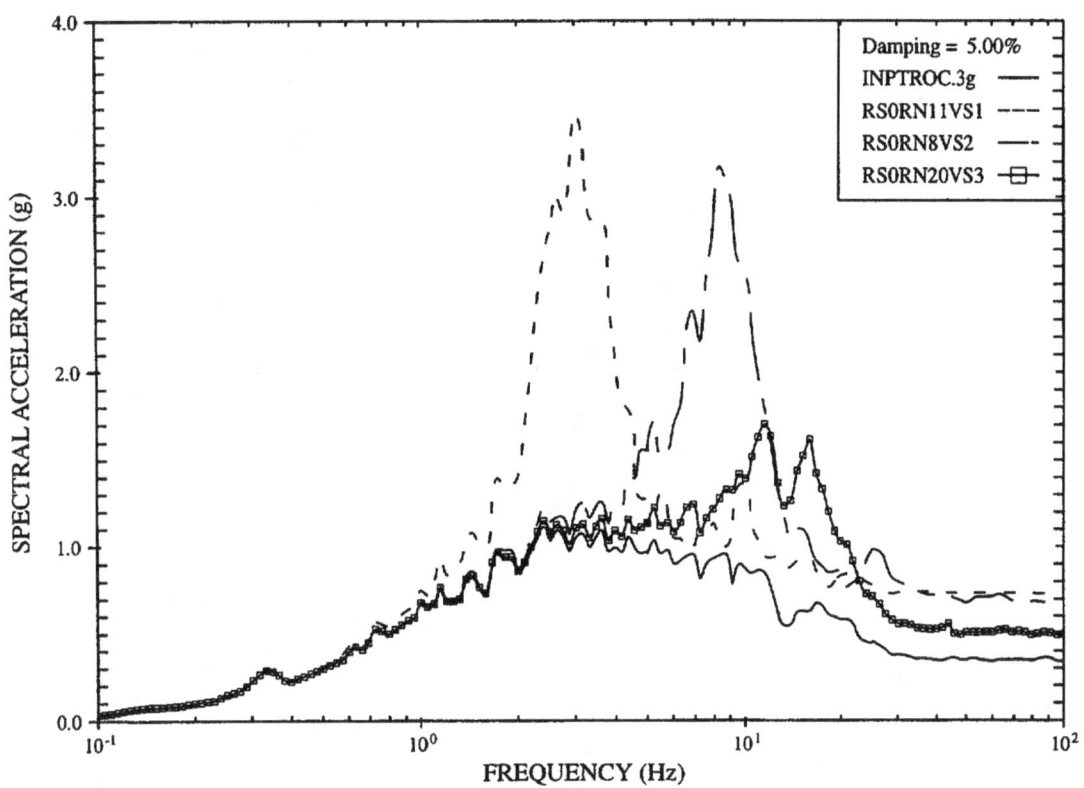

Figure 9. Effect of Soil Shear Wave Velocity, V_s, on Amplification at Ground Surface
(H=50ft; V_R=10,000fps) for R.G. 1.60 Input

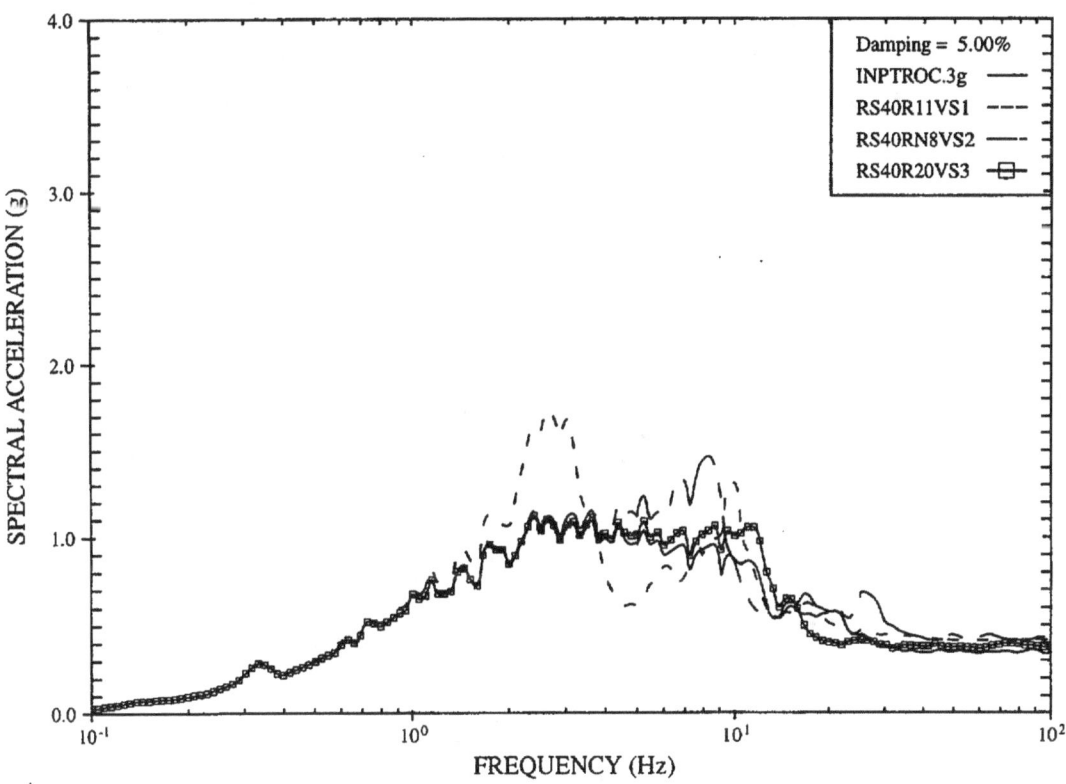

Figure 10. Effect of Soil Shear Wave Velocity, V_s, on Amplification at Depth of 40 ft
(H=50ft; V_R=10,000fps) for R.G. 1.60 Input

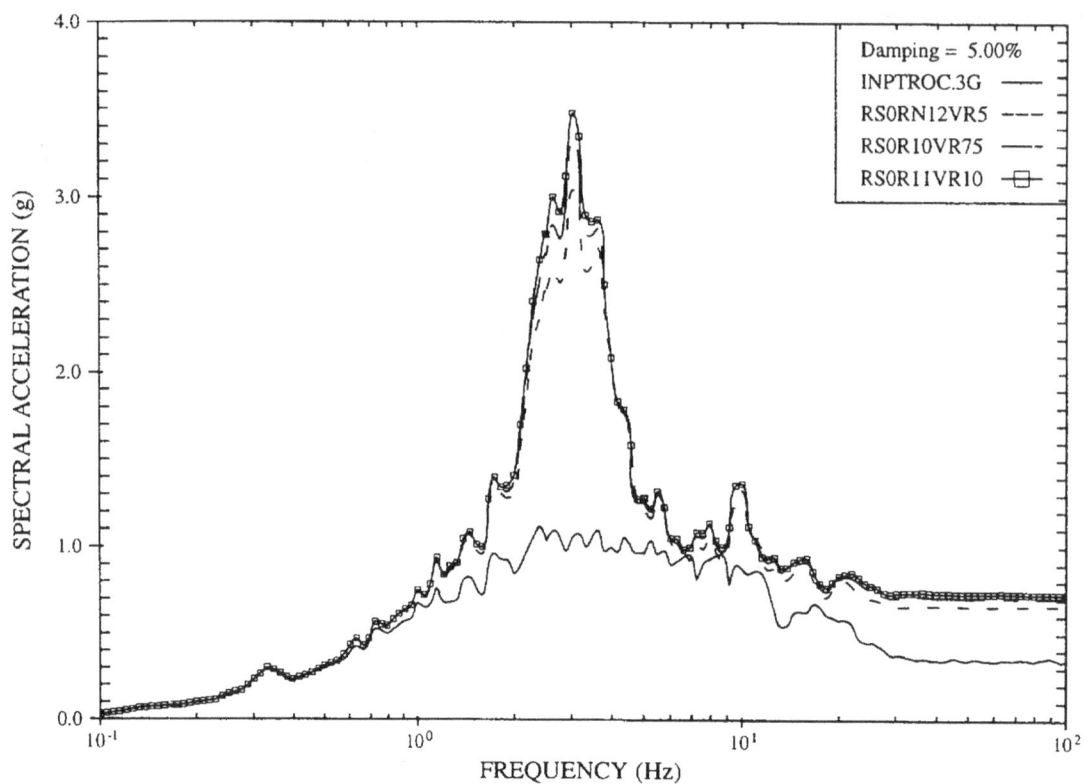

Figure 11. Effect of Rock Shear Wave Velocity, V_R, on Amplification at Ground Surface (H=50ft; V_s=1000fps) for R.G. 1.60 Input

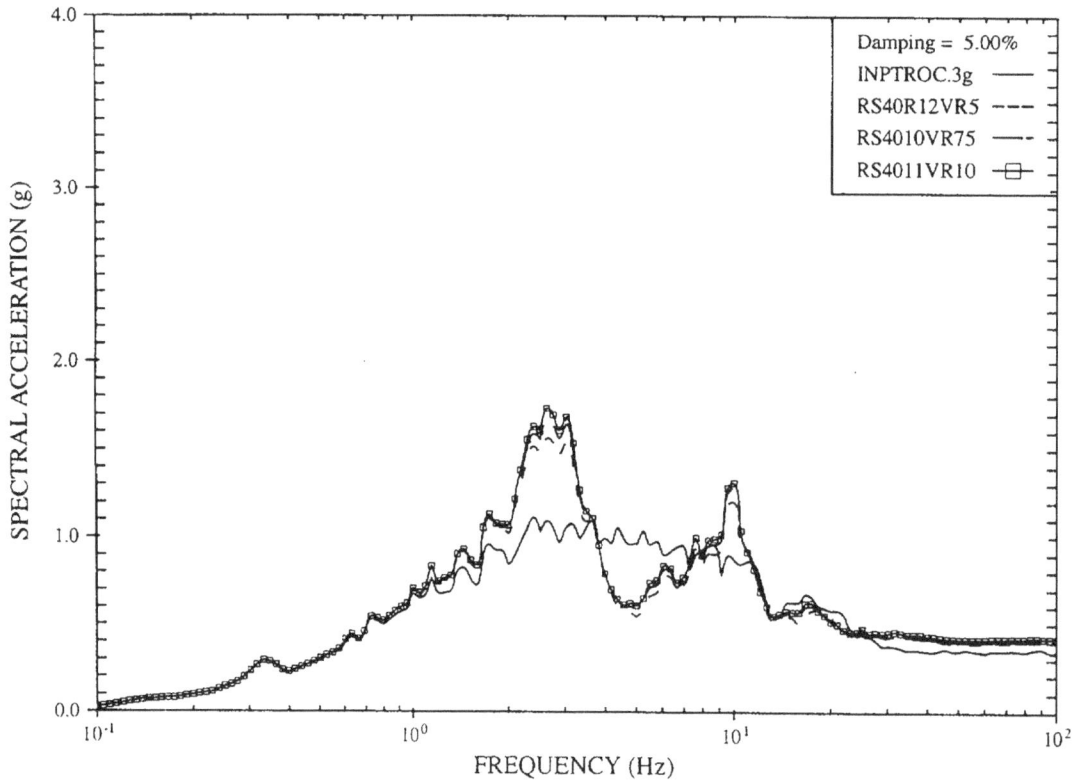

Figure 12. Effect of Rock Shear Wave Velocity, V_R, on Amplification at Depth of 40 ft (H=50ft; V_s=1000fps) for R.G. 1.60 Input

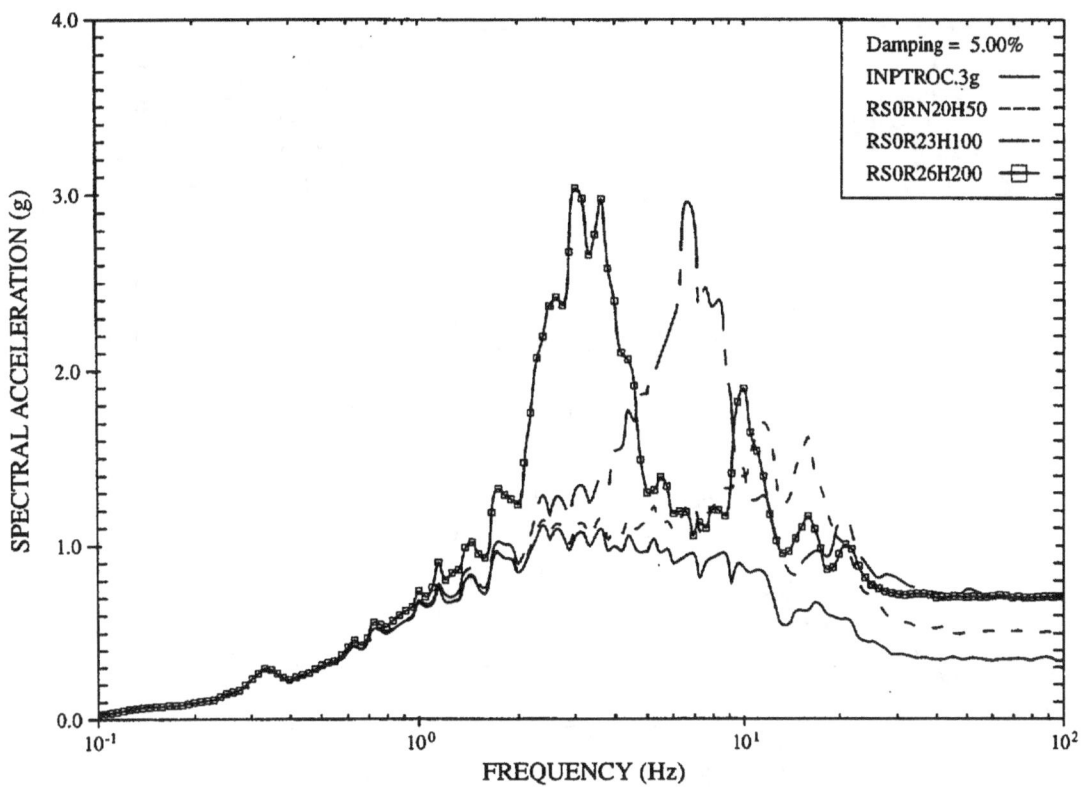

Figure 13.   Effect of Soil Thickness, H, on Amplification at Ground Surface
(V_s=3000fps; V_R=10,000fps) for R.G. 1.60 Input

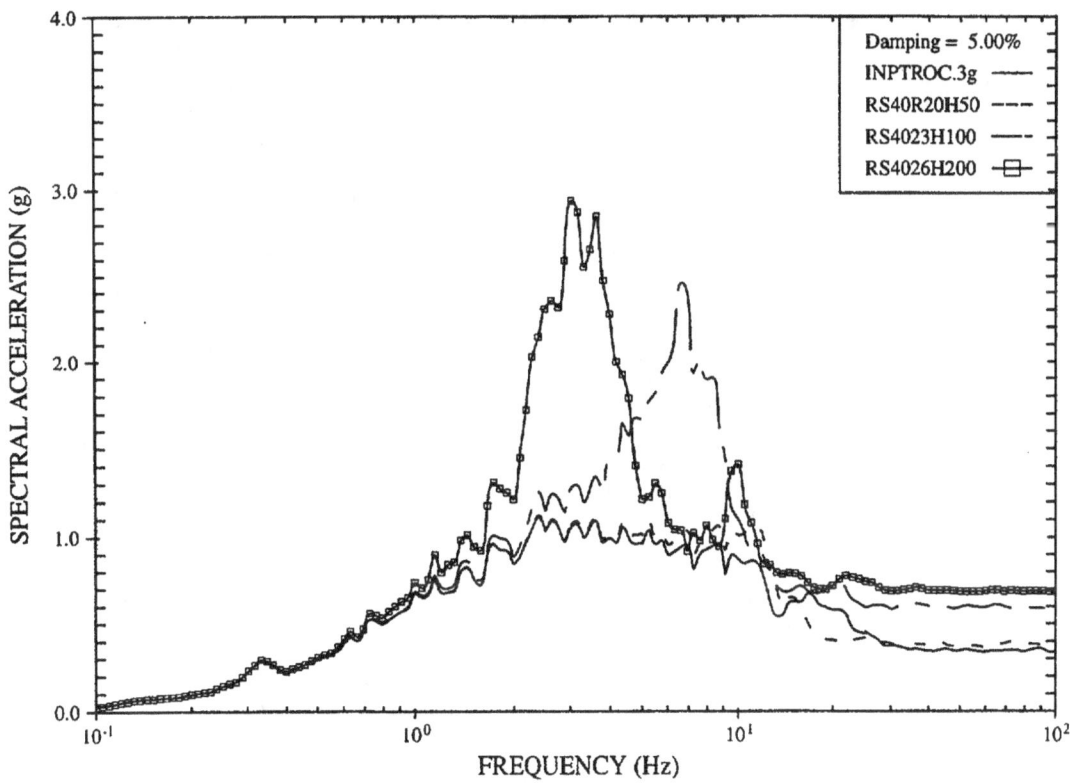

Figure 14.   Effect of Soil Thickness, H, on Amplification at Depth of 40 ft
(V_s=3000fps; V_R=10,000fps) for R.G. 1.60 Input

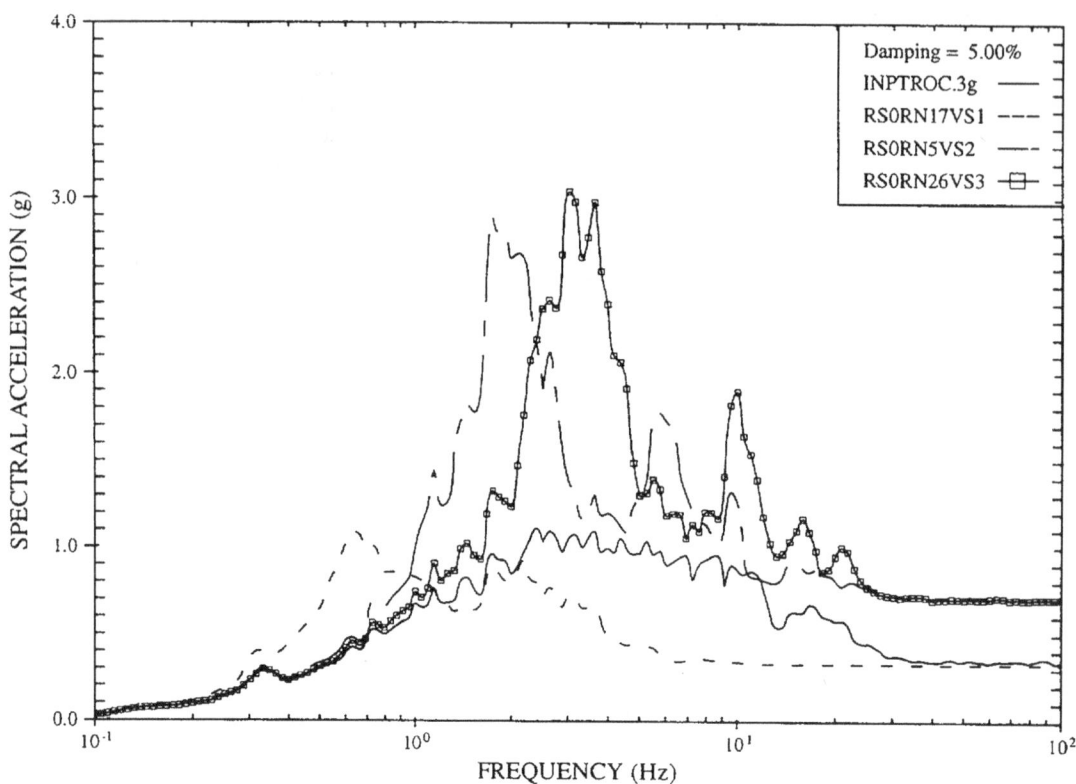

Figure 15.   Effect of Soil Shear Wave Velocity on Amplification at Ground Surface
(H=200ft; V_R=10,000fps) for R.G. 1.60 Input

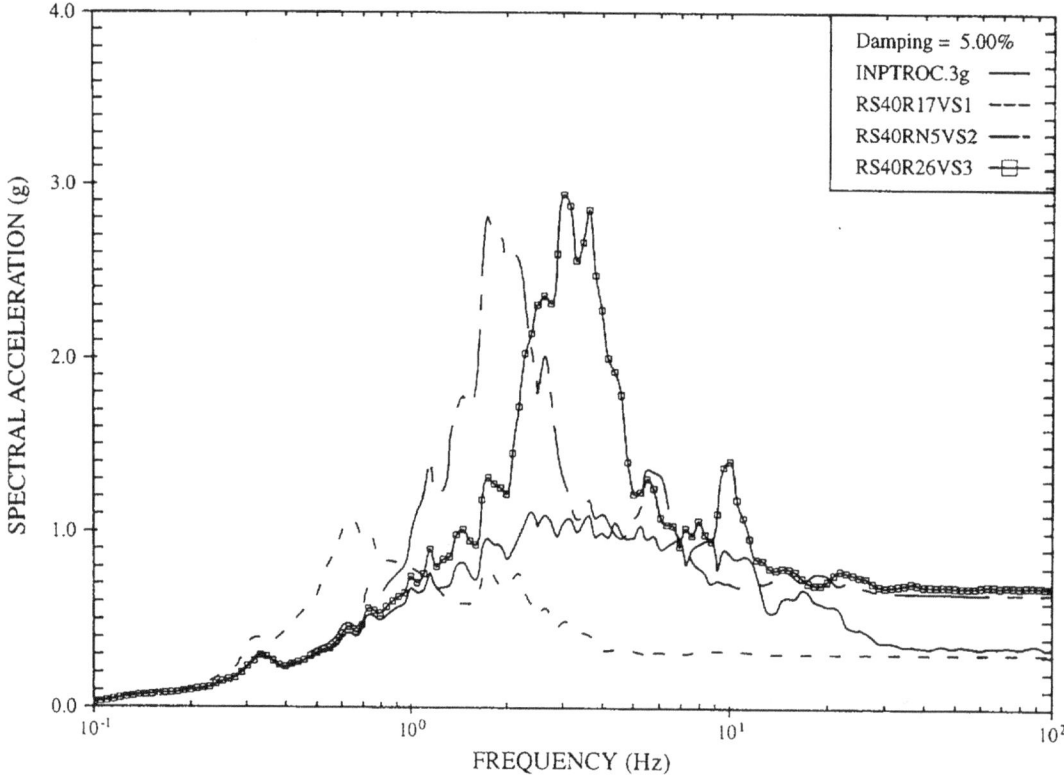

Figure 16.   Effect of Soil Shear Wave Velocity on Amplification at 40ft Below Ground Surface
(H=200ft; V_R=10,000fps) for R.G. 1.60 Input

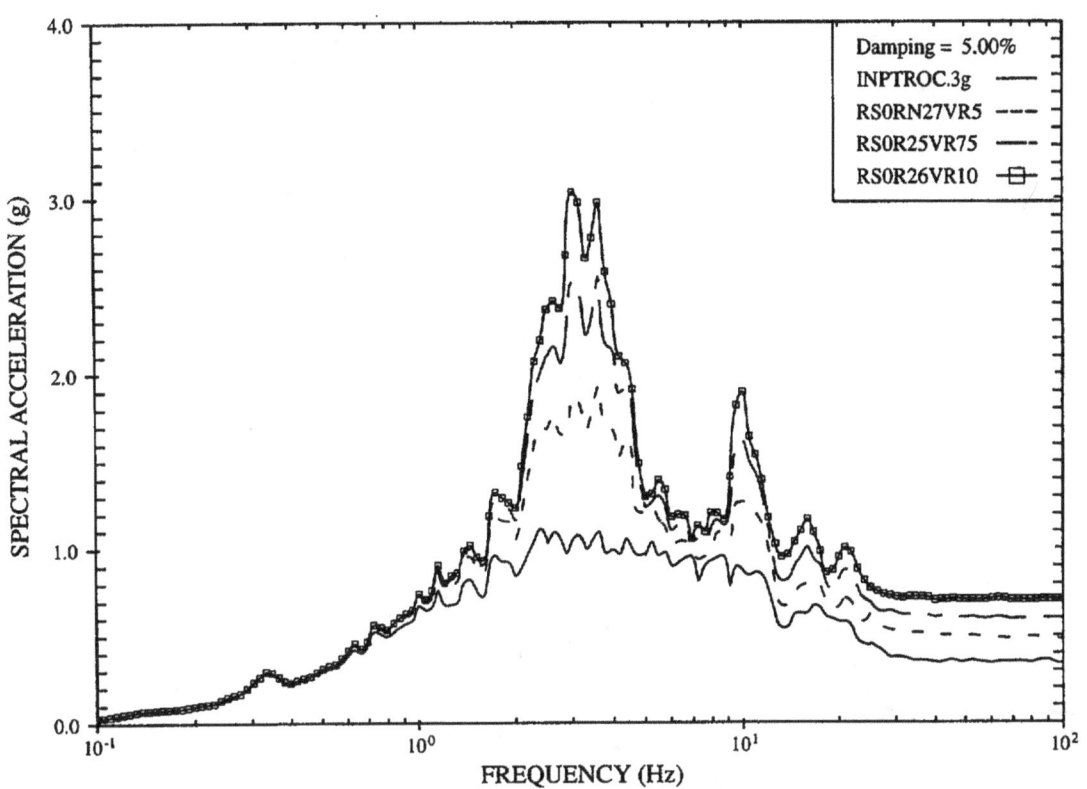

Figure 17. Effect of Rock Shear Wave Velocity on Amplification at Ground Surface
(H=200ft; V_s=3000fps) for R.G. 1.60 Input

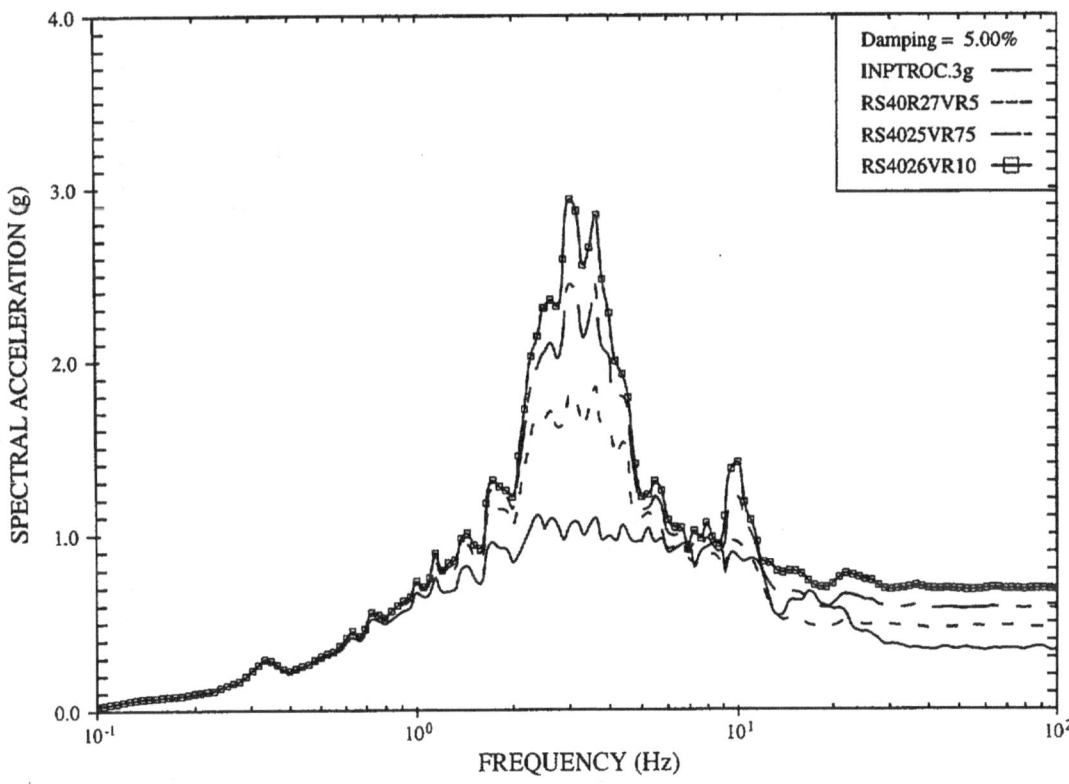

Figure 18. Effect of Rock Shear Wave Velocity on Amplification at 40 ft Below Ground Surface
(H=200ft; V_s=3000fps) for R.G. 1.60 Input

23

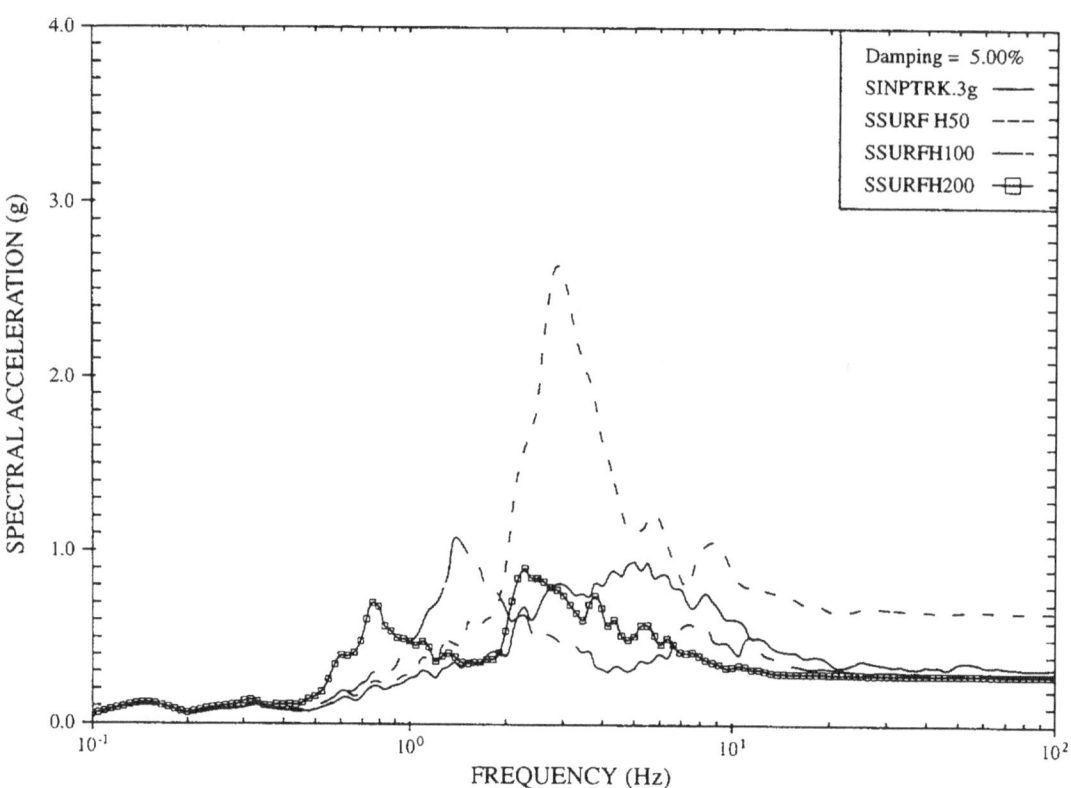

Figure 19. Effect of H on Amplification at Ground Surface (V_s=1000fps, V_R=10,000fps) for Rock Site-Specific Spectra Input

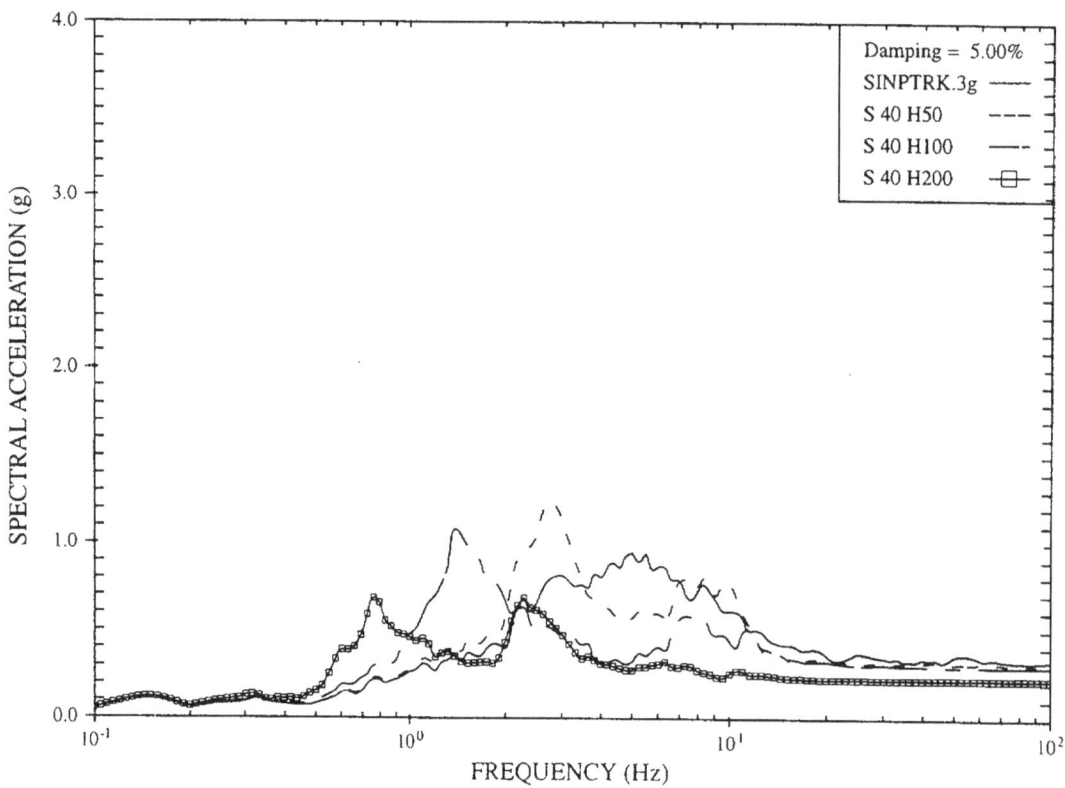

Figure 20. Effect of H on Amplification at Depth of 40 ft (V_s=1000fps, V_R=10,000fps) for Rock Site-Specific Spectra Input

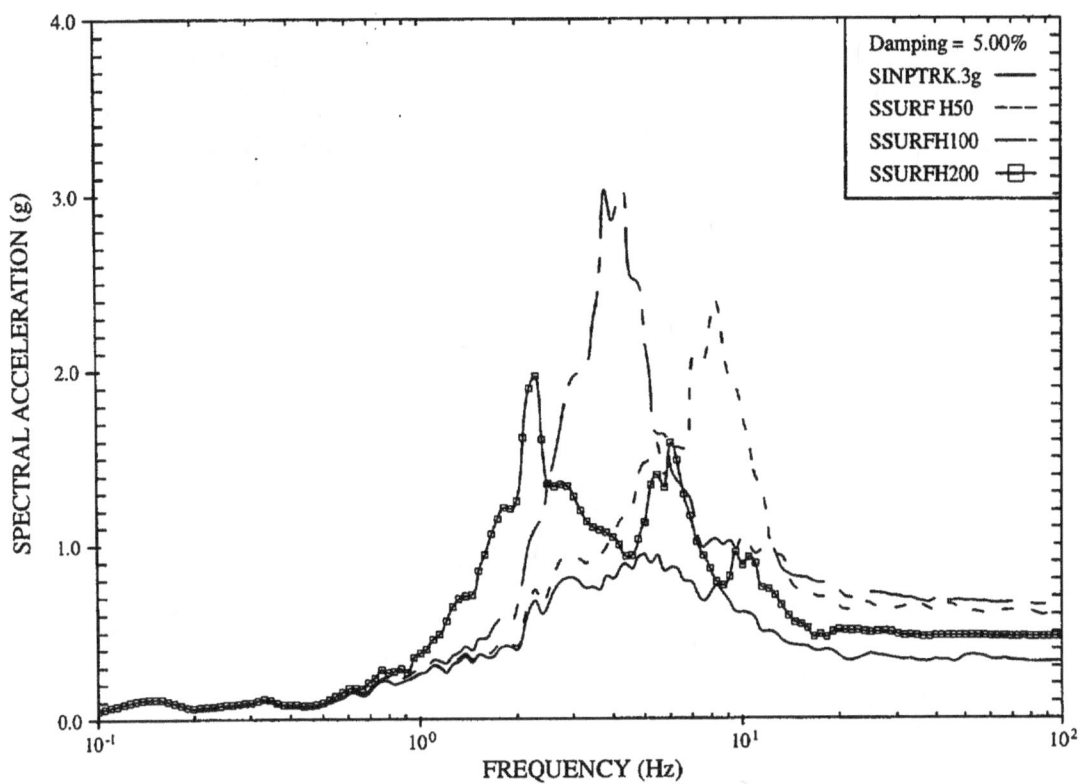

Figure 21. Effect of H on Amplification at Ground Surface (V_s=2000fps, V_R=10,000fps) for Rock Site-Specific Spectra Input

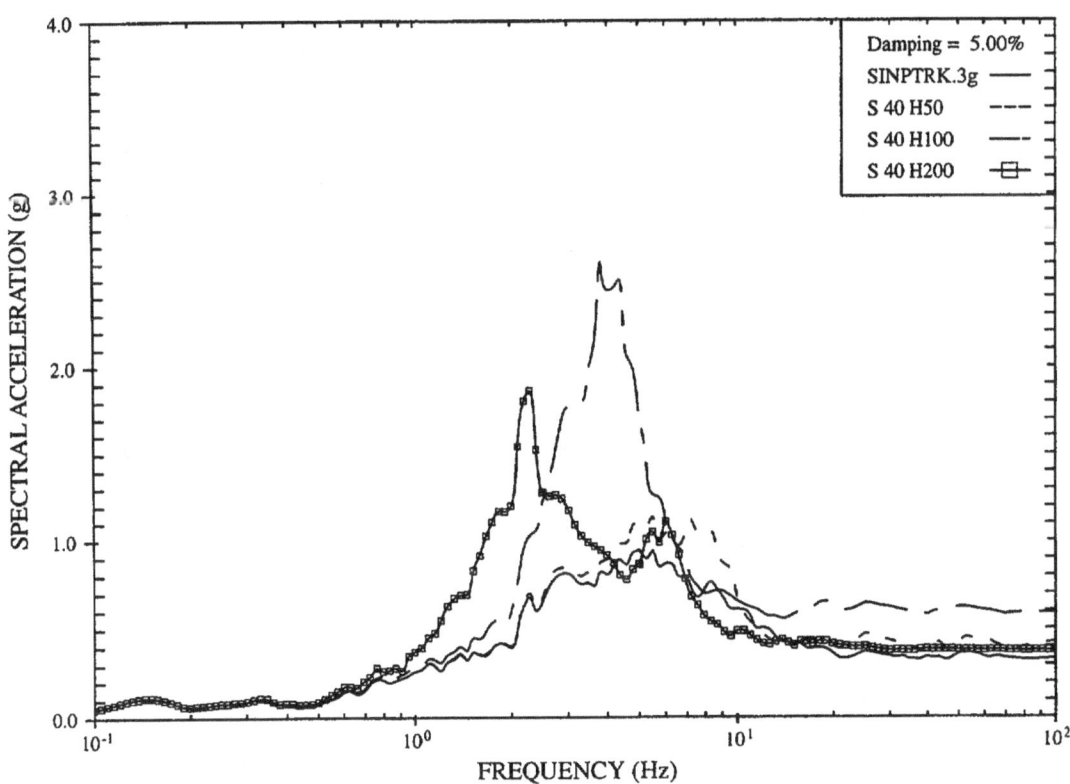

Figure 22. Effect of H on Amplification at Depth of 40 ft (V_s=2000fps, V_R=10,000fps) for Rock Site-Specific Spectra Input

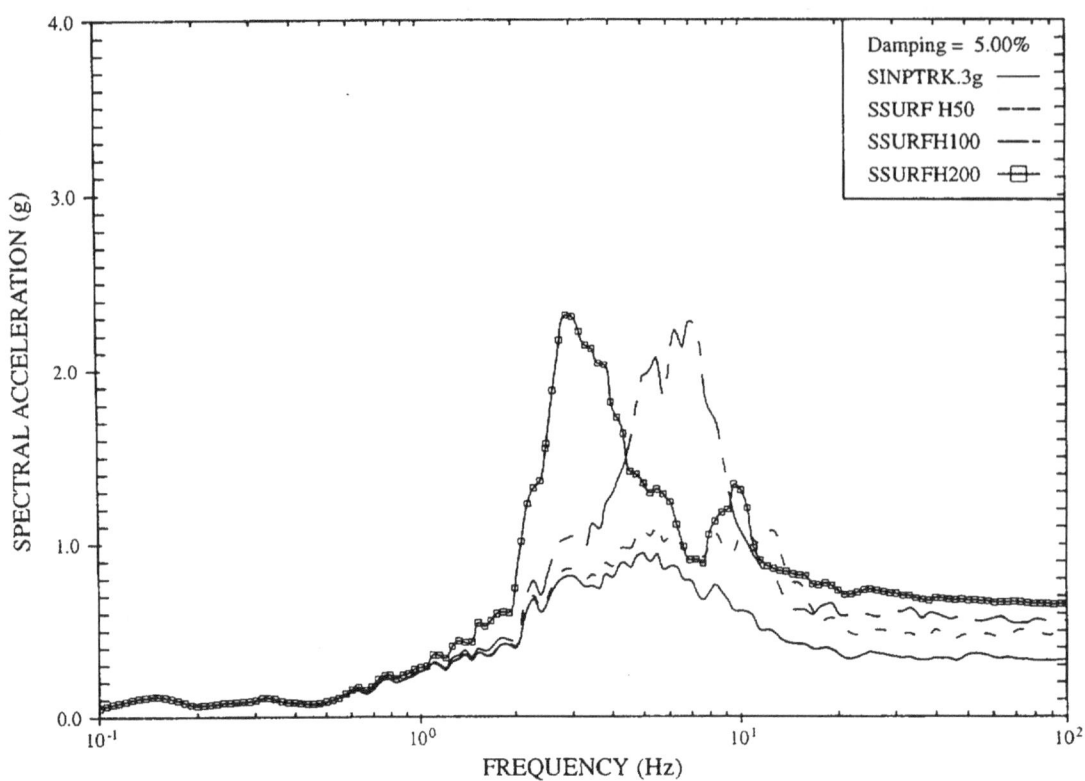

Figure 23. Effect of H on Amplification at Ground Surface (V_s=3000fps, V_R=10,000fps) for Rock Site-Specific Spectra Input

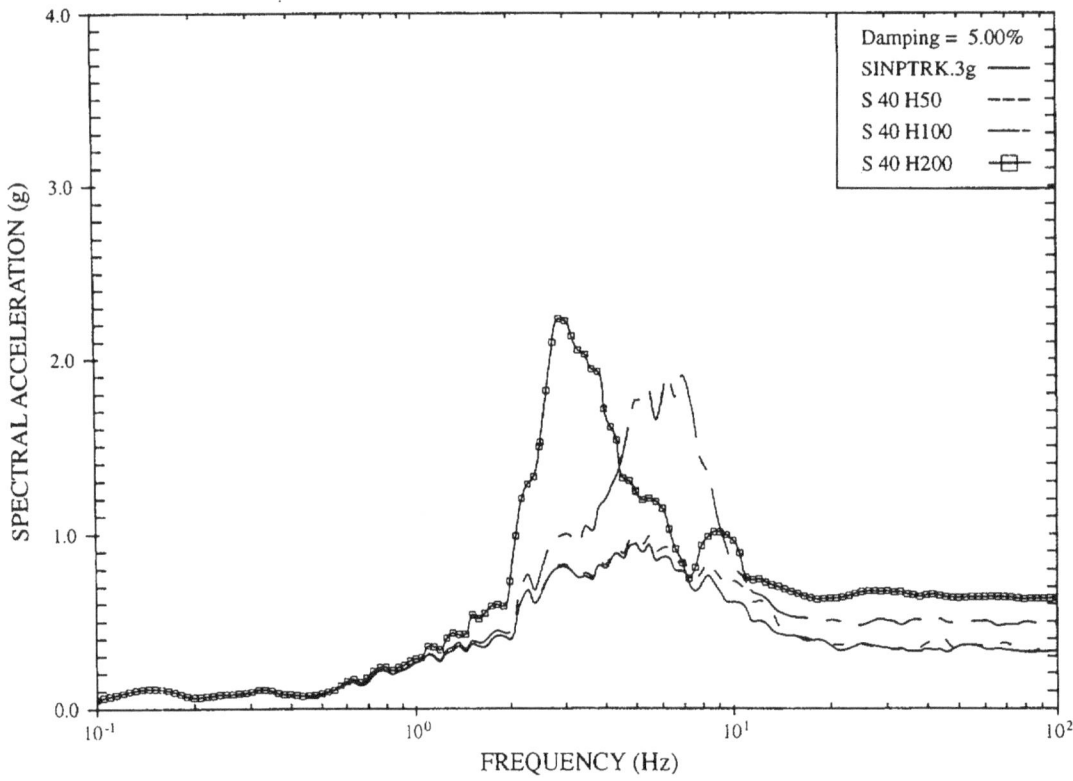

Figure 24. Effect of H on Amplification at Depth of 40 ft (V_s=3000fps, V_R=10,000fps) for Rock Site-Specific Spectra Input

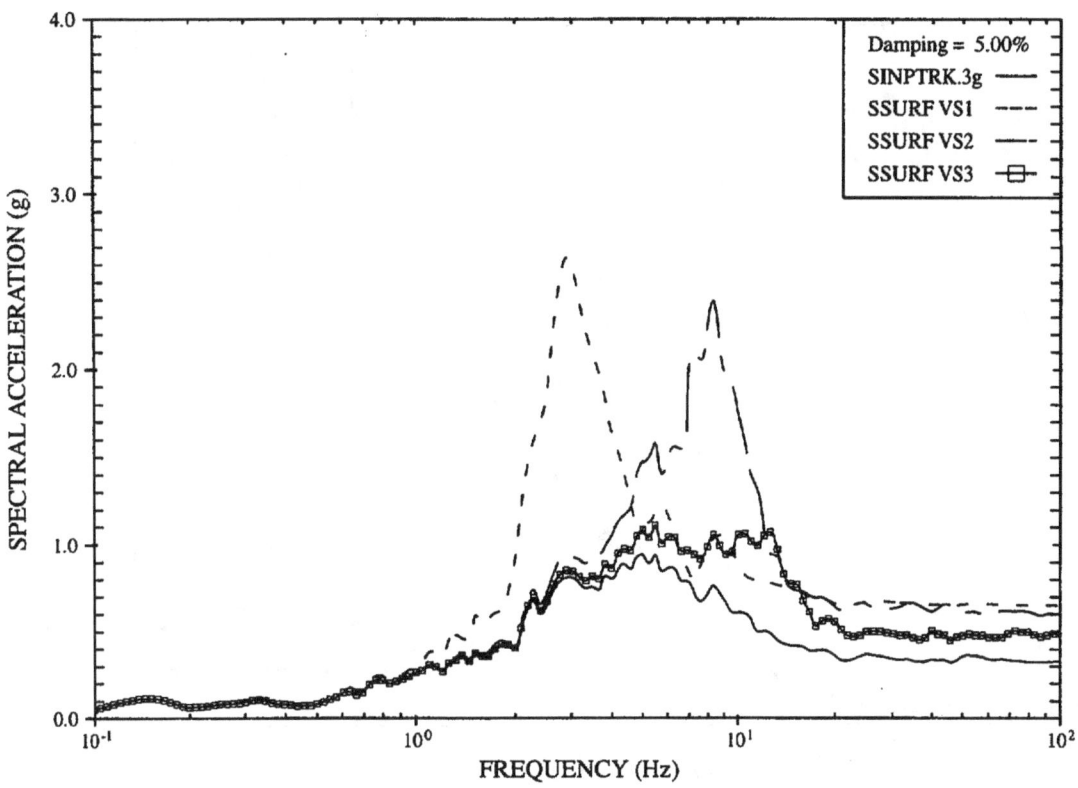

Figure 25. Effect of V_s on Amplification at Ground Surface (H=50ft, V_R=10,000fps) for Rock Site-Specific Spectra Input

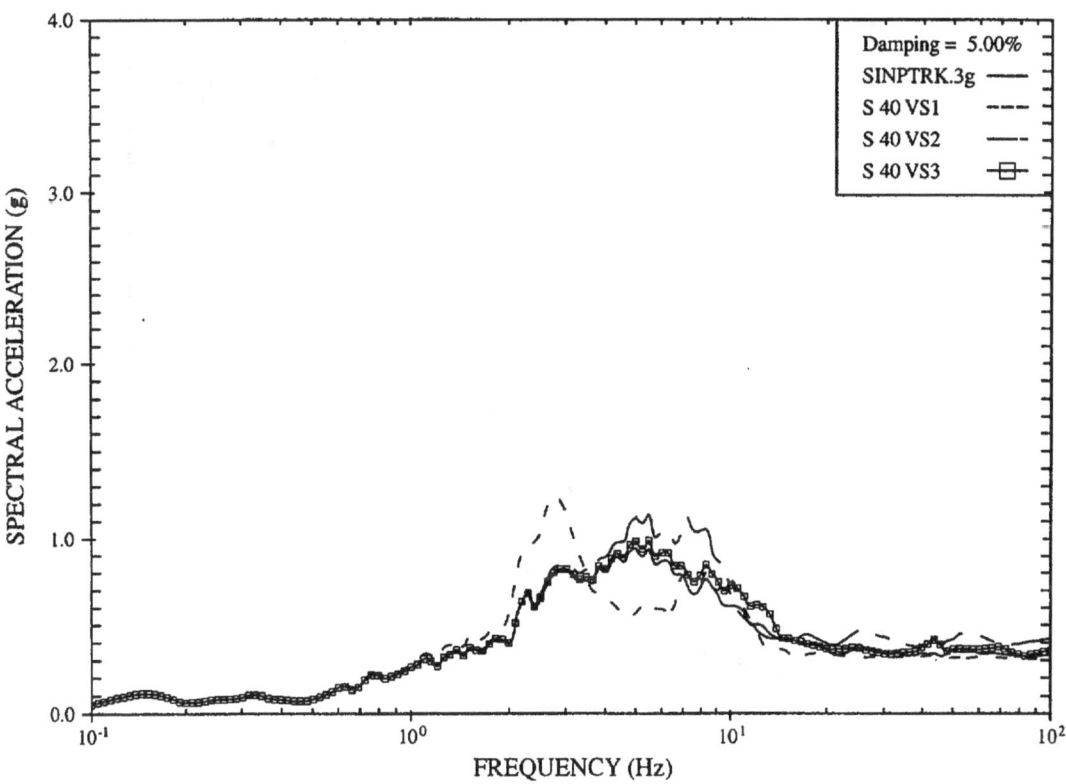

Figure 26. Effect of V_s on Amplification at Depth of 40 ft (H=50ft, V_R=10,000fps) for Rock Site-Specific Spectra Input

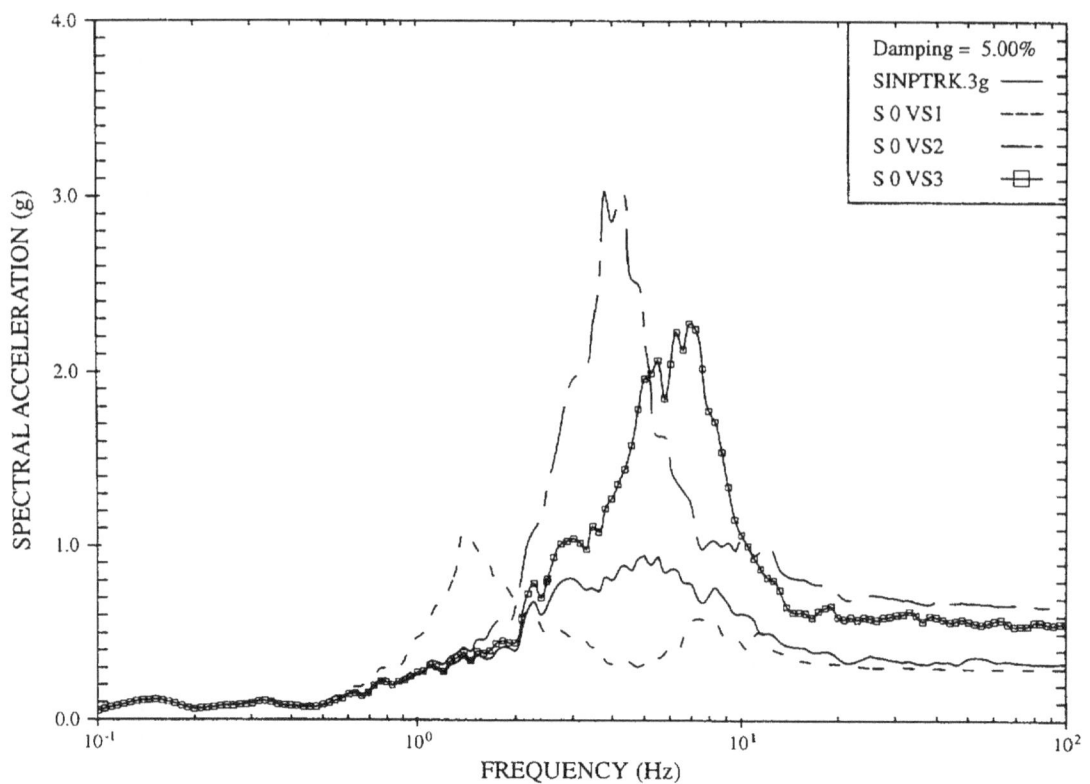

Figure 27. Effect of V_s on Amplification at Ground Surface (H=100ft, V_R=10,000fps) for Rock Site-Specific Spectra Input

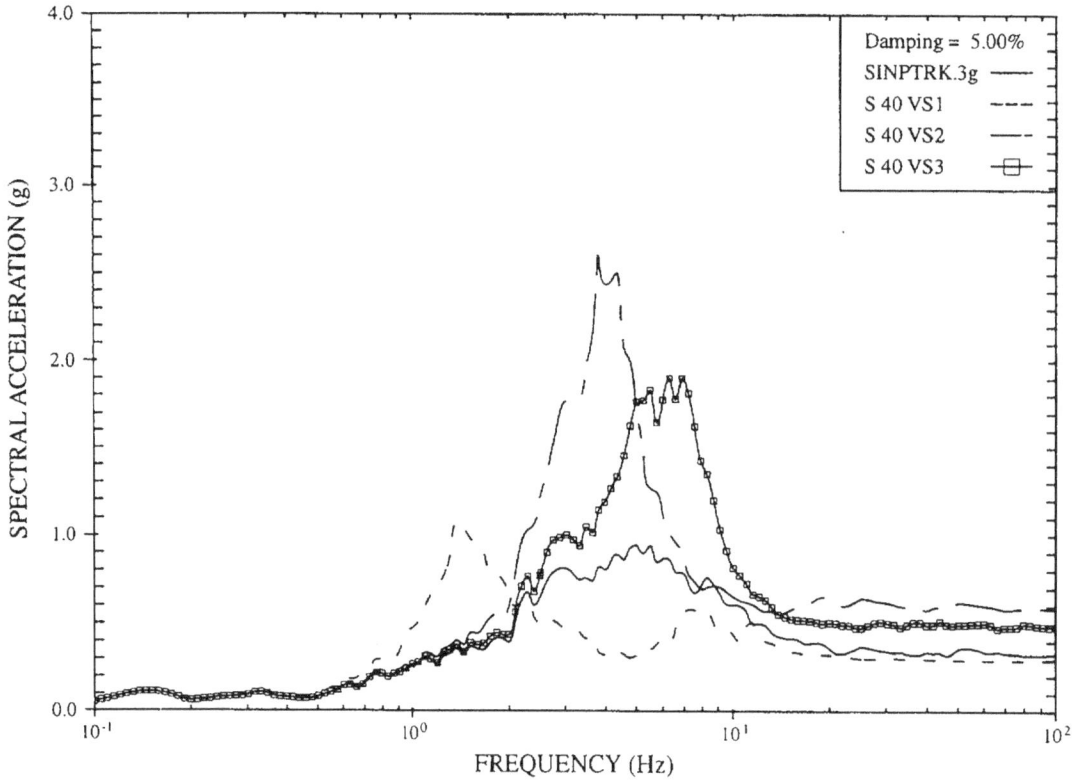

Figure 28. Effect of V_s on Amplification at Depth of 40 ft (H=100ft, V_R=10,000fps) for Rock Site-Specific Spectra Input

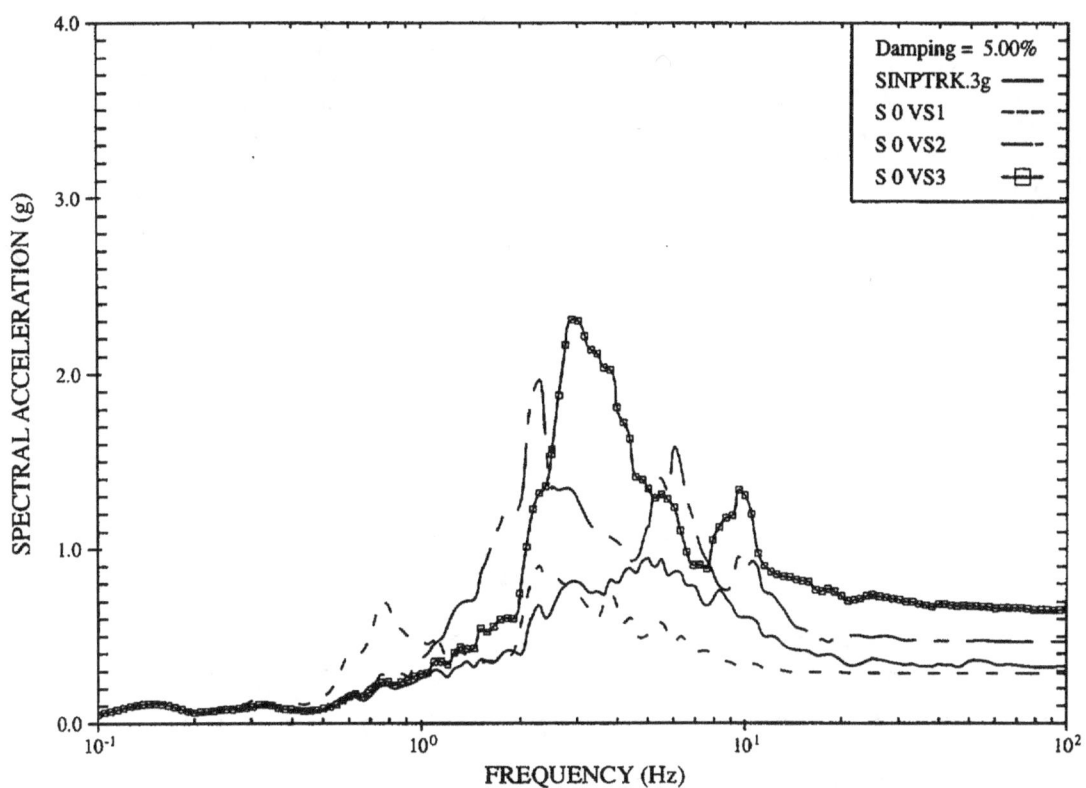

Figure 29. Effect of V_s on Amplification at Ground Surface (H=200ft, V_R=10,000fps) for Rock Site-Specific Spectra Input

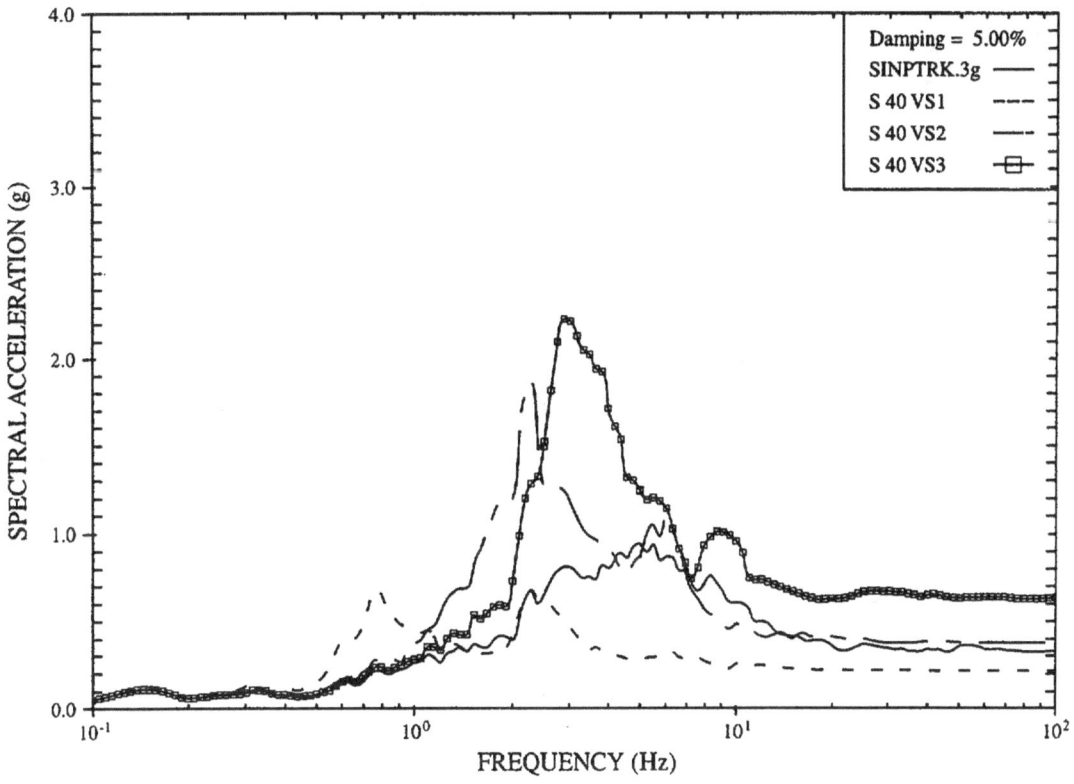

Figure 30. Effect of V_s on Amplification at Depth of 40 ft (H=200ft, V_R=10,000fps) for Rock Site-Specific Spectra Input

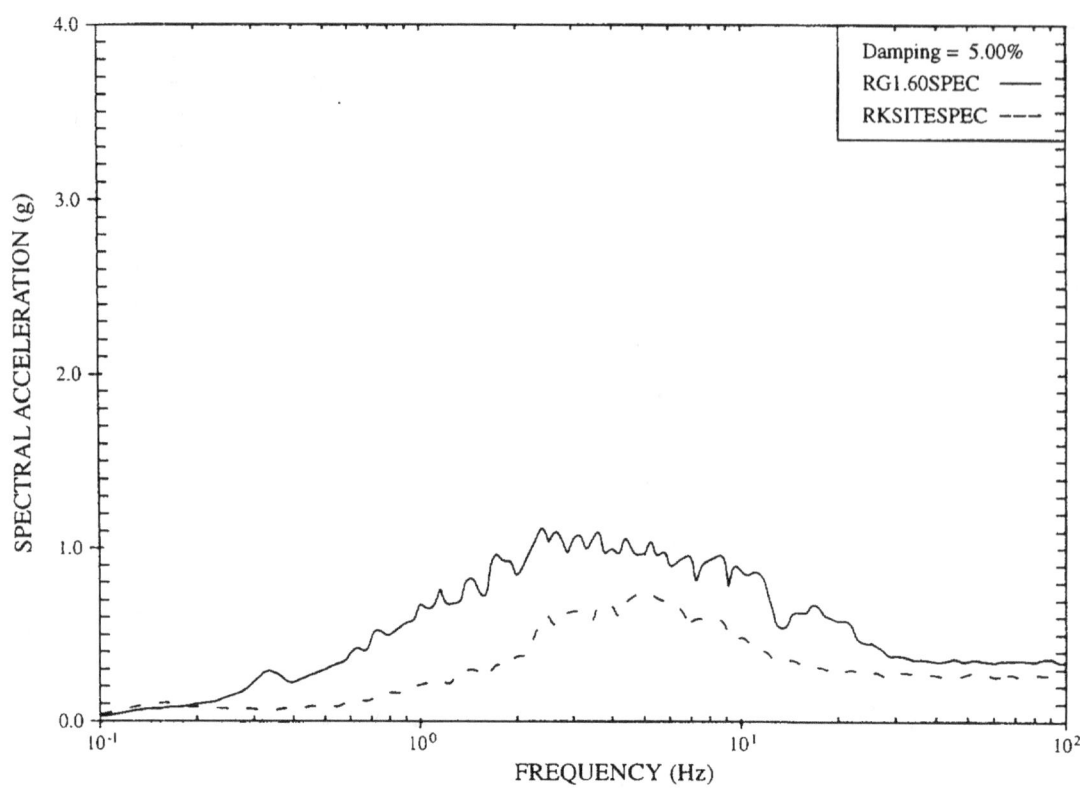

Figure 31.   Comparison of R.G. 1.60 Spectrum with Rock Site-Specific Spectrum
(with PGA of 0.3g for both input spectra)

APPENDIX: "CARES - Computer Analysis for Rapid Evaluation of Structures, Version 1.2,"
A Report prepared by Carl J. Costantino, Charles A. Miller, Ernest Heymsfield, and Anshi Yang.
(The report is in ADAMS Documentation Accession No. ML012670418).

NRC FORM 335 (2-89) NRCM 1102, 3201, 3202	U.S. NUCLEAR REGULATORY COMMISSION **BIBLIOGRAPHIC DATA SHEET** *(See instructions on the reverse)*	1. REPORT NUMBER (Assigned by NRC, Add Vol., Supp., Rev., and Addendum Numbers, if any.) NUREG-1750

2. TITLE AND SUBTITLE

Assessment of Soil Amplification of Earthquake Ground Motion Using the "CARES" Code Version 1.2

	3. DATE REPORT PUBLISHED

MONTH	YEAR
September	2001

4. FIN OR GRANT NUMBER

5. AUTHOR(S)

R. Pichumani

6. TYPE OF REPORT

Technical

7. PERIOD COVERED *(Inclusive Dates)*

8. PERFORMING ORGANIZATION - NAME AND ADDRESS *(If NRC, provide Division, Office or Region, U.S. Nuclear Regulatory Commission, and mailing address; if contractor, provide name and mailing address.)*

Division of Engineering
Office of Nuclear Reactor Regulation
U.S. Nuclear Regulatory Commission
Washington, DC 20555-0001

9. SPONSORING ORGANIZATION - NAME AND ADDRESS *(If NRC, type "Same as above"; if contractor, provide NRC Division, Office or Region, U.S. Nuclear Regulatory Commission, and mailing address.)*

Same as above

10. SUPPLEMENTARY NOTES

11. ABSTRACT *(200 words or less)*

This report describes the results of two studies to assess the soil amplification of earthquake ground motion by varying three parameters pertinent to the soil and rock supporting nuclear power plant structures. In the first study, the input earthquake ground motion (corresponding to the Regulatory Guide 1.60 spectrum) was specified at the rock level. The study analyzed the effects of varying each parameter on the motion at the ground surface and at 40 feet (ft) below the ground surface. The results of the first parametric study show significant shifts in the frequency at which the maximum spectral acceleration occurs when the soil thickness is varied from 50 ft to 200 ft and when the shear wave velocity of the soil stratum is varied from 1000 fps to 3000 fps. No frequency shifts are seen when the shear wave velocity of the rock medium is varied from 5000 fps to 10000 fps, but significant changes in the maximum spectral amplitude of acceleration are observed for the 100 ft and 200 ft thick soil layer. The second parametric study used the seismic ground motion specified by a rock site-specific spectra input at the rock outcrop. A comparison of the results of the two parametric studies shows that the shapes of the spectral responses for both types of ground motion input are quite similar to the corresponding cases of soil thickness and soil shear wave velocity. However, the spectral amplitudes obtained for the site-specific rock spectra input are lower than the corresponding values for the Regulatory Guide (R.G) 1.60 input because the amplitudes of the input spectral accelerations of the site-specific rock spectra are lower than those of the R.G. 1.60 spectra at all frequencies larger than approximately 0.18 Hz, even though the peak ground acceleration (PGA) of the site-specific rock spectra was set at 0.3g by scaling the actual PGA of 0.24g by a factor of 1.25 to match the 0.3g PGA of the R.G. 1.60 spectra.

12. KEY WORDS/DESCRIPTORS *(List words or phrases that will assist researchers in locating the report.)*

soil amplification
earthquake ground motion input
site-specific spectra
soil shear wave velocity
rock shear wave velocity

13. AVAILABILITY STATEMENT

unlimited

14. SECURITY CLASSIFICATION

(This Page)

unclassified

(This Report)

unclassified

15. NUMBER OF PAGES

16. PRICE

NRC FORM 335 (2-89)

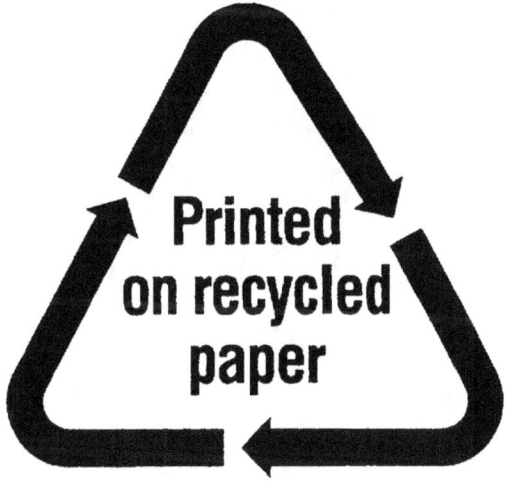

Printed
on recycled
paper

Federal Recycling Program

NUREG-1750

ASSESSMENT OF SOIL AMPLIFICATION OF EARTHQUAKE GROUND MOTION USING THE "CARES" CODE VERSION 1.2

SEPTEMBER 2001

UNITED STATES
NUCLEAR REGULATORY COMMISSION
WASHINGTON, DC 20555-0001

OFFICIAL BUSINESS
PENALTY FOR PRIVATE USE, $300